TWO WAYS OF
CARING

TWO WAYS OF
CARING

A BIBLICAL DESIGN
FOR BALANCED MINISTRY

WILLIAM E. HULME

AUGSBURG PUBLISHING HOUSE
MINNEAPOLIS, MINNESOTA

TWO WAYS OF CARING

Copyright © 1973 Augsburg Publishing House

Library of Congress Catalog Card No. 73-78270

International Standard Book No. 0-8066-1334-3

Scripture quotations unless otherwise noted are from the Revised Standard Version of the Bible, copyright 1946 and 1952 by the Division of Christian Education of the National Council of Churches, and are used by permission.

MANUFACTURED IN THE UNITED STATES OF AMERICA

Contents

Chapter 1

Growing Awareness of Imbalance

At the present time I am a teacher of pastoral counseling in a theological seminary and also director of a ministry in social change graduate program for a local consortium of seminaries. To some this may seem a strange combination. How can someone who has been in the pastoral counseling field be taking an interest in social action? To me they belong together. My interest in social action is as old as my interest in pastoral counseling.

During my last sabbatical leave I was able to do what I had been wanting to do for some time. I had been increasingly aware that pastoral counseling as a ministry to individuals, marriages, and families was incomplete in itself because the social and cultural context within which these individuals, marriages, and families were living was also contributing to their problems. Pastoral care would not be balanced until it also included in its ministry this larger environment. I used the sabbatical year to develop a program that would equip people to minister also to this social and cultural context within which we live.

The ministry in social change program that has resulted is

not a substitute for counseling with individuals, marriages, and families, but a needed complement to such counseling. In fact, counseling ministries are included along with social action ministries in the field work assignments of the program. In either ministry—counseling or social action—we are involved in pastoral care.

Two Experiences from Student Days

My conscious awareness for the need of this balance in ministry, these two ways of caring, goes back to two experiences as a seminary student. One concerned an uncle who had suddenly become mentally ill. I visited him several times during his stay in the hospital and was frustrated by my inability to communicate with him. Having read what I could on the subject I developed an interest in pastoral counseling and subsequently entered into graduate studies in the field.

The other experience concerned my teaching of a Sunday School class of boys in a slum area of the city. I had little support from the families of these boys and had to contend with the fact that no one would be arousing them on Sunday morning. In desperation I took on the responsibility myself and left an hour early to go from house to house, often entering the room where the boy was still asleep. I have never forgotten what one of the boys told me on such an occasion. In his usual cooperative manner he thanked me for my interest, but advised me to forget about him. Evidently he had had a bad night or a bad week. "It's no use Bill," he said. "You can't be a Christian and live in this neighborhood."

His obvious sincerity moved me to feel with him in his discouragement. I could wake him up on Sunday morning and hopefully persuade him to get dressed and come to Sunday School. There I could teach him about Christ and the Christian way. But what could I do about this blighted environment in which he had to live? I realized then that poverty was more than a lack of material goods. It was an overpowering social force that distorted and stunted the lives of those who were trapped under its weight.

Early Experience with the Courts

A few years later I was approached by one of these boys when I was a pastor of a congregation in the same city. He was in trouble with the law—charged with "rape with consent." This was the legal way of stating that he had had sexual intercourse with an underage girl. He came to me because he needed my help when his case came to court. He repeated his only justification of his behavior several times: "I didn't know that she was that young!" When I asked him if he were aware that his behavior might be questioned from a Christian point of view even if the girl were of age, he seemed honestly bewildered. So I talked with him then and there about sex and its meaning in human relationships.

Later when I appeared with him and his parents in court, the judge deferred the case until he could be examined by a psychiatrist. This was the last he ever heard from the court. He never saw a psychiatrist nor was his case ever reconvened. This was my first experience with an overburdened and inadequate court system. It has been established that the verdicts of our courts function as deterrents to law violations only when they are given without undue delay. While the boy's act could scarcely be called a crime, the action of the court was similar to the inconsistency in authority that he had known all of his life. What impression did this experience leave on him of our social order? of established authority? of responsible behavior? What kind of support did it provide to my discussion with him about sex?

Environmental Frustration of Sex Education

Instruction in sex is itself an example of the need for accompanying social action. Preoccupied with sexual stimulation, our culture works against the kind of attitude and self-direction in regard to sex that we would hope to communicate in sex education. The business and entertainment worlds exploit sex for their own lucrative purposes and provide a counter education. Take the so-called double standard as a case in point. From a Christian perspective men and women are equally responsible for their sexual behavior. Our society, however, has long been structured on an assumed differentiation between the sexes and only the woman was expected to be responsible. Now with the sexual revolution the situation is changing. The double standard is being abandoned but in a direction opposite a Christian perspective: neither the man nor the woman is expected to be concerned about any limitations in sexual behavior. Our movies both document this change and promote it.

Putting all of our pastoral efforts in the area of sex into teaching and counseling when the social context within which people live is frustrating our purposes is inefficient to say the least. Are there not other ways of reacting to this distorted environment than by the traditional retreat from it into isolated communities or by the equally traditional attack on it with puritanical censorship? Why has it taken a woman's liberation movement to put together an effective corporate protest against the sexism of our culture?

10

Plea Bargaining Substitute for Jury Trial

One of the clergyman students in our first class of the ministry in social change graduate program developed an interest in the court system because of experiences similar to my own. In his field assignment with an urban Indian center he became curious over why he was spending so much of his time in jails and courts. Was the Indian so much more of a law violator than his own middle class white? Or are we as a society more inclined to jail the poor and the minority peoples than the white and affluent peoples?

After studying the record of the criminal courts of our two countries over a two year period he came up with some disquieting statistics. Although the great majority of people who were charged with crimes were subsequently found guilty, only a minority of them had had a jury trial. Why? Because a jury trial takes time and there were simply too many cases. The alternative time saving plan has been accomplished through "plea bargaining." By charging the accused with a number of related offenses, he is faced with a longer sentence if convicted. However, if he will plead guilty to one of the charges or to a less serious offense, he is relatively hopeful of receiving a lighter sentence. His case then is quickly dispensed with by the judge without the long tedious chore of a "trial by one's peers."

While it helps to perpetuate a system that is no longer adequate, plea bargaining not only can be used to intimidate the innocent, but also can make it possible for some who should be confined for their own and society's sake to be released after a relatively short period of time.

In counseling with those charged with criminal offense, whether in jails and prisons or as they await trial or subsequent to their release, we need to take into account a system of justice that for all of its effectiveness is also inclined to jail the poor more than the affluent, to rely on plea bargaining to manage its docket of cases, and to submit a person to long delays between arrest and trial. For the poor this time of waiting is often spent in jail, since the bail system obviously favors the affluent. To maintain a balance in our caring for the offender, we need to care also about this system: it needs to be changed!

With the Poor in the Rural Slum

My experience with the lot of the poor was further augmented when I began my career as a teacher of pastoral counseling in a theological seminary. In addition to my courses in pastoral counseling in which the students ministered under supervision in hospitals and correctional institutions, they desired also to minister within the community. We selected the place most in need of attention—a shantytown outside the city limits where there was no school, church, or public institution or building of any sort. We began with the traditional approach of a daily vacation Bible school, followed by attempts to organize a youth group. Soon we realized we were up against a cultural impasse.

The people of this rural slum were outcasts as far as the larger community was concerned; they were quickly labeled in the public schools to which they were bussed and in employment opportunities and tended to live up to expectations. We discovered we could not really minister to the people as individuals or even as families apart from ministering also to the social structures that had distorted their self-image. To do this we needed to *live* in the community.

The student pastor assigned to the task had completed a quarter of clinical pastoral education at a state prison. When he began living in the community he realized he was ministering to people with problems similar to those of the people in prison, but now he was in the social context out of which these people came and into which they returned. In this context it was not enough to counsel persons in their needs and to assist them in adjusting to their environment. In living with them the student became concerned about the kind of social context in which these people lived and about ways and means for changing it.

The community had no sense of identity. With the help of our denomination we erected a community building in which religious services and other activities could take place. This provided a focus for identity. No person in the community had ever graduated from high school. One of the first programs we put into effect in the new building was tutoring for the children still in school. But this was not enough. We visited the school officials and teachers of the city to inform them of what we were attempting to do and to enlist their cooperation. In these ways we gradually broke through the negative image projected by the schools on these children. There was no recreation facility in the community for the children. With assistance from a city service club we erected a playground. But this was not enough. We had to carry on a running battle—ultimately victorious—with the State Highway Commission to lower the traffic speed for the children's safety in reaching the playground.

In the spring we had a hepatitis epidemic. We informed the public health officials but they were content to dismiss it as a logical consequence of poor sanitary conditions. We learned how to apply pressure on these officials to secure the needed inoculations of the people, using the community building as a temporary clinic. The people's attitude toward effort and enterprise was as negative as their self-image. They needed positive experiences to overcome their apathy. So we secured a vacant field, persuaded nurseries to supply us with tomato plants, and then sold the tomatoes to local markets with sufficient profit to purchase a second-hand school bus for community transportation needs. When we formed circles to celebrate Holy Communion we could sense the developing spirit of community.

The Poor and the American Work Ethic

One of the field assignments in the ministry in social change graduate program is with a church located in a housing project where the maximum annual income permitted for occupancy is $3500. The first student involved in this assignment became aware of the same deflated self-image among the people of the project as we encountered in the rural slum. On the basis of his research he developed the thesis that the American work ethic has been the principle standard by which particularly the man in our culture estimates his self-worth. According to this ethic a man's worth is based on what he does for a living and his success in it. In our socio-economic system this striving for success becomes highly competitive. The poor for various reasons lose out in this competition. Their loss is not only in material benefits of success but also in the positive esteem that our culture bestows on it.

In the past, the church's attitude toward the poor was one of charity. Collections of food and clothing and even of money were given to them. During the depression of the thirties government welfare programs began to take over this function. What was intended by the government as a temporary relief to assist persons to get "back on their feet," has become a permanent institution. With their charity role toward the poor considerably reduced, the more affluent church people, in the absence of any meaningful contacts, have developed an antagonism toward the poor. People on welfare are often scorned because they *don't* and supposedly *won't* work for a living. So the poor who are already deprived of self-esteem by the work ethic are now rejected by this same standard.

A recipient of the church's charity did not improve his self-image, but he was at least the object of care. Even this small asset may be lacking when one is the recipient of an impersonal government welfare program.

The antipoverty programs that developed in the sixties in which the poor were given a voice in their administration were a major step forward in the promotion of self-esteem. When the poor are taken into the decision making processes, when they *share* the *power,* the programs are structured on the basis of mutual respect. The conflicts that have followed because of this structure may not have been anticipated. Perhaps some of the architects had hoped that in gratitude for a voice the poor would use this voice in an agreeable way. But freedom to decide makes the decision itself unpredictable.

The church as an institution and as individuals in society has a responsibility for shaping the corporate structures of society. Since mutual respect is an essential attribute of Christian relationships, the church's influence in this aspect of the anti-poverty programs is hopefully evident. Yet the old charity approach to the poor conferred on the giver more status than on the receiver. Though something less than the goal of mutual respect in which each can give and receive *something,* the charity approach was far closer to it than our present antagonism which reenforces our societal polarization.

Because of the nature of its message the church may be a polarizing influence, but only because its position is an offense to some. It can never be true to itself when its polarizing influence is due to the attitudes of its own people in their rejection of others whom they find offensive. By the very nature of its message the church's role is directed toward reconciliation and not polarization, because it is the church of *Christ* in whose life, death, and resurrection the love of God for all people is expressed. The church's love, therefore, is for *all* our neighbors and not just those we prefer. In reference to the individual this means that we bind up our neighbor's wounds as the Samaritan did to the one who fell among thieves. In reference to the social context this means that we use our influence for social justice as Amos did when he protested to the power structures that the poor were being sold for a pair of shoes.

The Scope of the Endeavor

It is out of my concern that we express our care in both of these ways that I write this book. In the following chapter, I shall point out some hopeful signs that the church is taking its responsibility for social justice more seriously than it has in the past. The history of the church (in America in particular) has been characterized by a chronic resistance to its responsibility for the social order. We will examine some of the specific causes for this resistance unique to the American scene.

Our religious tradition, however, is oriented toward a ministry to society in the function of the Old Testament prophets. We shall compare this prophetic function with that of the Old Covenant priest in his concern for reconciliation with God as illustrative of the need of both of these ministries. The church has been hindered in its priestly and prophetic functions by its identification with the clergy at the expense of the laity. We shall give our attention to remedying this situation.

Our present problems in church and society are to a large degree an inheritance from the decades of the fifties and early sixties in which the church in America reached its crest in popularity. The acculturation of the church that accompanied this popularity in many instances has played its role in the present trends toward social polarization. We shall reflect on this golden age of the church, giving special attention to the acculturation process.

The prophetic way of caring is needed to reverse this process. Our problem is not whether we have the power to affirm the Christian position in opposition to cultural values but whether we can tolerate the conflict that ensues when we do. The answer is indicative of how emancipated we are as congregations and as individuals to function as God's change agents. We shall take the position that we are responsible to God for the use of this power as we are for the other "talents" he has provided for us.

On this basis we shall attempt to demonstrate that the use of this power needs to be applied to both the priestly and prophetic ways of caring, not only because both are needed for a balanced ministry, but because a person's priestly ministry becomes distorted if he does not also function as a prophet, and his prophetic ministry becomes distorted if he does not also function as a priest. Although each person and perhaps even each congregation has a more natural affinity toward either the priestly or prophetic direction, each needs also to maintain the other to become a better priest and a better prophet. By applying this same illustration of mutual benefaction to the congregation we shall attempt to resolve the apparent contradiction between the church as a retreat from the world and as a task force for changing the world.

While the church obviously has a past and has just as obviously been influenced by this past, it has often been unsure about whether it has a future. This has been particularly true during times of turbulence and change. Our anticipations then have been of the imminent coming of the Lord. Yet these very periods are also times of great opportunity for the church to influence the direction of change. Our final attention will be given to exploring this opportunity. With the hold of the assumptions and traditions of the past shaken, the future is wide open.

For the church to "seize the moment" it needs to affirm the priestly and prophetic ways of caring. As an institution in society the church is part of the establishment. At the same time it is critical of all human institutions, including its own. The tension between these two stances is the tension of being *in* the world and yet not *of* the world.

Chapter 2

The Church's Concern for Social Justice

During a speaking tour of the United States, Dr. Mikko Juva, President of the Lutheran World Federation, emphasized the changes that have taken place in this denomination. "Lutheranism," he said, "elevated the quest for social justice from its previous rather subordinate position and placed it as one of the central tenets of Christian ethics." Furthermore, it has "dissolved the centuries-old alliance with the conservative political forces, without, however, concluding any corresponding alliance with revolutionary forces."

Regarding social justice, he said, "Individual sins have always been castigated in Lutheran churches but very little has been spoken in most pulpits about the injustice social structures and the necessity to correct them through corporate social and political action." After the Lutheran World Federation Assembly at Evian, France in 1970, Juva says that "there can be no doubt about it that the Lutherans consider the struggle for social justice and the work for the diminishing of the gulf that separated the privileged and the underprivileged as one of the most urgent tasks the churches are facing today."

A New Emphasis

This change in the direction of social justice is a change toward the corporate dimension of the church's mission. Social justice refers to the social structures of society—the context—within which the individual person, the married couple, and the family live. This context—these structures—can be a root cause of problems, of illness, and of evil, even as such a cause is also within the individual person.

Traditionally, Christians have identified three sources of evil and its temptations: the devil, the world, and our own flesh. The devil represents a cause outside of human responsibility. Our own flesh is a cause within individual responsibility. The world is more complex. It represents a cause both within and outside of individual responsibility. On the one hand the individual is a contributing cause to the social structures that he and other individuals of the community construct. On the other hand he is also a creature of these structures. They can enhance or depress his individual capacities for development.

The power for change inherent in the Christian message and implicit in the church's mission applies to each of us as individuals, and also to the structures that we build in our society.

A Lesson from the French

The changes that Mikko Juva described had taken place previously in many other Christian bodies. One of the most forthright statements on the church's responsibility for social justice was made recently by the French Protestant Federation. Though it is a small church body, comprising less than two percent of the population of France, the influence of its twenty-six page document already has gone far beyond its own numbers. An initial edition of 12,000 copies was quickly sold out.

The document is the result of eighteen months of study and deliberation by a group of churchmen. The report states unequivocally that "the economic and political powers in place, that is, the system and ideology which structure the society in which we live, are unacceptable in their present state." The reason is to the point: the domination and manipulation of the weak by the strong in such a society is "radically incompatible with the Gospel."

The document goes on to state that the socio-economic order can only be changed by political action and that it is precisely this kind of action that the church should take. The risk involved in confronting the forces of power needs to be accepted.

Upon receiving the report the secretary general of the French Protestant Federation, Albert Nicolas, said, "for a long time our churches profited from this society and its advantages. They did not want to see reality. We no longer have the right to remain silent" (*Christian Century*, March 8, 1972, p. 274).

In what in the eyes of some has come close not only to "breaking the conservative political alliance," but also to "forming an alliance with revolutionary forces," the World Council of Churches in September of 1970 initiated a financial program to combat racism. Funds were offered to liberation movements, most of which are in that part of Africa still under white domination. Some of these movements, according to reports, are engaged in guerilla activities that include violence.

The Council could anticipate a reaction, and it came from many parts of the world. In the United States a roving editor of *Reader's Digest* took up the cudgels. Clarence Hall in the October 1971 issue asks, "Must Our Churches Finance Revolution?" Maintaining that supporting violence is in contrast to the church's mission, Hall concludes: "Does the present ardor of the World Council and some of its member churches for political, social, and economic revolution merely betoken errors in judgment made by well meaning but naive Christian leaders? Or are these the moves of desperate men who are no longer sure what their mission is, and have lost faith in orderly change and in the potency of Christianity's age old weapons—reconciliation and love—which over the ages have again and again transformed both men and their societies?" (p. 100).

Hall's attack did not go unanswered. The Excutive Secretary of the World Council's New York office, Eugene L. Smith, issued a "Statement on Two *Reader's Digest* Articles," October 1971. The funds, said Smith, were given for humanitarian purposes, earmarked specifically for health, welfare, and educational programs. Charging that Hall lifted much of his evidence out of context and distorted his report by what he omitted, Smith affirmed the Council's resolution that racism is "a blatant denial of the Christian Faith," and "one of the world's basic problems." The financial grants, he said, were the means of putting this resolution into action. Smith concluded by exposing what he felt was Hall's obvious bias: he did not report the opinion of any Black African!

One is reminded on a global scale of Jeffrey Hadden's sociological research among American churches entitled, *The Gathering Storm in the Churches*. It is the storm of conflict between institutional leaders—often clergy—who initiate programs for social justice and in so doing irritate others—

often laymen—who see in such programs an attack on the very structures they deem essential for a stable society.

Some denominations, as well as some individual congregations whose concerns have long been for social justice, are experiencing their own reactions. As one veteran "social activist" pastor put it, "I'm beginning to wonder whether all of our attempts to effect change in society have really accomplished anything more than a weakening of our own base of operation."

Alliances—Pro and Con

Breaking an alliance with "the conservative political forces," as Dr. Juva states, without forming any "corresponding alliances with revolutionary forces," places any church in a good position to function in a way consistent with its own identity. Churches have been "burned" in their alliances. The alliance with conservative political forces has alienated many in the past who have felt oppressed by the political and economic structures of their society and have identified the church with the oppressors.

An example of another kind of alliance is the one that the social gospel minority and their successors in the churches formed informally with the organized labor movement. These social activists believed that the labor movement was the needed ally for bringing about social justice. I was a graduate student at a liberal theological seminary during the latter days of that alliance, and picketing in a local strike was the counterpart to demonstrating in anti-war or civil rights causes today.

Now, however, in "coming of age," organized labor has undergone a change. With higher wages, shortened work hours, higher pay for overtime, better working conditions, and more guarantees for worker rights, the movement has lost some of its fire for social justice. In fact, some unions have been guilty of a breach in social justice by resisting the inclusion of minority peoples into their ranks.

The recent resurgence for social justice in some areas of the church has been closely associated with the civil rights movement. The integration of the races was part of the goal, and integration is obviously a feature of Christian neighborliness. Now, however, some of the allies in later forms of this movement are calling for the separation of the races. In the National Black Political Convention held prior to the political party conventions in 1972, for example, the controversial issue was the submission of a preamble that endorsed black separation. This has created a tension in the ranks. Nonviolence had been accepted as the means to secure civil rights. Now some of the allies are defending and even threatening violence as a justifiable means. This created another tension.

The prophets in the Old Testament warned the people of Israel against forming alliances. Because of Israel's vulnerable position among the nations, these alliances were usually military in nature. It was a temptation, for example, for little Judah to seek an alliance with big Egypt as a defense against the rising power of aggressive Babylon. The prophet's concern was that such alliances would compromise Israel's uniqueness among the nations. The prophet thought alliances displayed a lack of trust in God to care for his people. If through Moses he could save them from the Egyptians at the Red Sea, he could save them also from the Babylonians.

The church like Israel is a different kind of social entity. It is and it is not one societal institution among others. It is also *Christ's body,* figuratively speaking, and therefore has transcendent dimensions. Its orientation is the Christian heritage of which it is the embodiment, and not liberal or conservative predispositions, alignments with labor or management, capitalist or socialist socio-economic structures or militant or moderate attitudes toward effecting change. The church's goals and its methods in its care for social justice can never be identified with any political, economic, or social movement, nor in its care for the individual, with any therapeutic movement.

The increased concern for social justice at the level of national and world federations of churches has not reached the grass roots in many local congregations. It is at this base that our efforts need to be directed. The elevation of the quest for social justice is a welcome swing of the pendulum following the *turned-inwardness* of the church in the previous decades. Yet it contains the potential for its own imbalance. The quest for social justice cannot in itself be identified as the church's way of caring. Rather it is a complement to another way of caring . . . caring for our own varied needs as persons in the congregation as well as for similar needs of individuals outside the congregation.

Chapter 3

Coping with a Chronic Difficulty

The church today has a two-pronged task: to minister to *society* in terms of social justice and to *individuals* in terms of their specific needs. Yet the church in the United States has had a difficult time harmonizing these two emphases. Either we concentrate on individual persons, marriages, families, and congregations in their needs, or we concentrate on the social order as the deficient context within which these individuals, marriages, families, and congregations function. The latter concentration, however, has occurred much less often than the former.

Historical Conflict

American church history shows a continual conflict between those who would save individual souls and those who would save society, between those who seek to meet the needs of individuals, marriages, and families and those who would change societal structures. In his book, *Righteous Empire,* church historian Martin Marty traces this conflict from the colonial era to the present. During this span the Protestant churches, in their concern for establishing a righteous empire in the United States as a "new covenant" type of promised land, have been dominated by the evangelicals with their emphasis on individual salvation and personal piety. Their concern for society was largely limited to the influence each converted person would exert in his day-to-day living. Yet few if any guidelines were offered to him other than the usual code of personal morality: abstention from the traditional vices in alcohol and sex, charity toward the poor, honesty and thrift in behavior, and concern for the salvation of others.

The rewards for adopting this model for behavior were associated with life beyond the grave, but as the churches adjusted to American society and began to identify it with the righteous empire, these rewards took on also temporal significance. The development of the American work ethic during this era is one result. A converted person would be expected to show his new life of obedience by his willingness to work for a living. Resistance to work was associated with the sin of sloth. If one worked hard he could expect God's blessing on his efforts. Financial security was one such blessing. Sloth brought the opposite, poverty, as its "just reward."

The predisposition to identify American democratic society with a Protestant empire tended to diminish the gap in the believer's perception between the kingdom of God and the values and ideals of his own culture. Yet the *protest* of the Protestant was still there, although it was never able to take the lead. There were valiant attempts on the part of some to arouse the conscience of the church to the injustices of society and to the necessity for change in these social structures. Their voices were heard and their efforts had some effect. Yet the emphasis on individual salvation continued to hold sway.

Marty believes that the American experiment in the separation of church and state has tended to divorce the faith associated with the institutional church from the political, economic, and social structures of American society. Desirous of maintaining their freedom as a religious institution, the churches made an informal agreement with these other sectors of society: You stay out of our bailiwick and we will stay out of yours. Finding themselves locked in by such a "contract," the churches either withdrew from society or adjusted to it. As churches adjusted to society, their awareness of the gap between that society and the kingdom of God was lessened. It is easy to accept as good these structures to which one has grown accustomed. The pot, of course, is sweetened as such adjustments become profitable.

The Catholic immigrants had the most difficult time making the adjustment. The Irish arrived early and had a common language tie. They "made it" even to the presidency of the United States. Those from central and southern Europe found it more difficult. Although they were foreigners in the righteous empire, they too have finally made it. Only those whose skin pigmentation makes them highly visible have not become part of the mainstream of American life. Chief among these, of course, are the blacks.

The struggle of the blacks to enter the mainstream of American life has dominated the social scene in our recent history. Those white Americans whom the blacks have found most resistant to their demands for equality, particularly in the cities of the north, are often Catholic ethnic groups who have only recently "made it" in American society. To the superficial observer it may seem that those who were themselves the victims of prejudice are now the most prejudiced.

Liberal social critic Michael Novak, however, sees the situation differently. As one "born of the PIGS—Poles, Italians, Greeks and Slavs"—he believes that the "white ethnic" is forced to bear the brunt of the changes made to achieve racial integration. Yet he himself has had no share in the onus of slavery and subsequent segregation of blacks. As Catholics, non-Anglo-Saxons and laborers, they also knew what it meant to be "outsiders." Having finally adjusted to the American system they are now angered and confused by the changes being made in that system.

"Racism is not our invention," says Novak. "We did not bring it with us; we found it here. And should we pay the price for America's guilt? Must all the gains of the blacks, long overdue, be chiefly at our expense? Have we, once again, no defenders but ourselves?" ("White Ethnic," *Harper's,* Sept. 1971, p. 48). One of their own, Vice President Spiro Agnew, has been exercising more than simply an ethnic clout. Those who resonate to his position go beyond the ethnic.

In spite of the changes in the American scene, the old-line Protestant churches have never succeeded in bringing these two emphases of ministry to the individual and ministry to society into a simultaneous ministry. The strongest trend in ministry to society prior to our recent emphasis was the Social Gospel movement of the early 20th century. Spearheaded by Walter Rauschenbusch, a theological professor of social ethics in the old German Baptist denomination, the attempt was made to apply the social principles of Jesus to an industrialized society. Child labor and other untenable working conditions were attacked. The alliance, therefore, with the labor movement was a natural.

The Social Gospel movement stimulated a violent reaction among the evangelicals. To them it was another gospel— and therefore *anathema*—or cursed (1 Cor. 16:22). The polarization reached a new extreme. Some tried to mediate. They preferred to talk about the social implications of the gospel as a corrective to the Social Gospel. In spirit they

30

were more with the evangelicals than their opponents, and their concern was more for mediation than for social justice. Unfortunately their mediation permitted an intellectual ascription to a social emphasis without an accompanying commitment to social action. While polarization can be ostensibly lessened by vocabulary changes, the real test for reconciliation is in commitment to action.

The temptation continually before the churches is to endorse one emphasis or the other: either to put their efforts into a ministry to individuals or to put them into a ministry for social justice. The Social Gospelers could be extreme as the evangelicals. Marty points to Rauschenbusch as an exception to this polarization. In the midst of the polemics that engulfed him, he continued to locate the source of evil in the individual as well as in society—in the "flesh" as well as in the "world." Normally the polemics that ensued were sufficient to drive each "side" to polarized extremes.

Evaluation of Corporate Structures

Corporate structures are necessary for people to live together in community. Whenever people live close enough to each other to be aware of the other's presence, structures of corporate living will evolve. The important issue is not *whether* we will have structures for corporate living, but *what kind* of structures we will have. These need to be evaluated.

How do we evaluate such structures and by what standards? The churches already have their standard. Jesus called it "the law of love." Applied to our social setting it could be described by the phrase in our pledge of allegiance: "with liberty and justice for all."

As products of our social or community context, we can

31

be hindered as individuals in our development by this context. The cultural values that we internalize may not be conducive either to emotional health or spiritual growth. If you are a man, for example, you have been influenced by our society's image of masculinity. Since big boys don't cry, you learned early to keep your tender feelings to yourself. Not only your prestige but at critical moments even your safety may appear to depend on it. Also you became aware early of the necessity to compete—physically at first, athletically, and also intellectually.

Instead of growing out of such pressures, you grew into them. You became the adult male in a socio-economic rat race. By this time, also, the "image" was reinforced by a religiously oriented work ethic. Now the pressure is to succeed at your job so that you will move up the ladder. Here again competition makes us concerned primarily for ourselves. The connotations of such success take on an increasingly materialistic image, measured by the salary scale.

As a result of this cultural male image, the man in our society may evolve not only with a distorted sense of values but with a mind and body that show wear and tear of the destructive nature of these values. Not only is one judged a failure if he fails to achieve the image of a successful competitor; ironically he can also be a failure if he succeeds. The sacrifices in other areas of life that are demanded by the pressures of the "image," are made at a tragic cost to his person.

The woman is no less subjugated to distorting pressures by our social structures. Women's liberation movements are exerting a strong influence on society precisely because many women have felt stifled in their development as persons.

As shapers of our social context, we may be supporting corporate structures that benefit us at the expense of others.

The inequities of such structures become obstacles to personal development. If you live in a suburb, for example, the corporate structures favor you at the city dweller's expense. Suburbs have assumed rights that have little basis in "liberty and justice for all." They depend on supposed boundary lines to relieve them of responsibility for the larger urban area. Through local zoning ordinances they have been amazingly successful in limiting their population to their own selected segment of society. Although the suburb is dependent on the city and in many ways is its parasite, its property taxes as well as other sources of revenue remain with the suburb. So the city grows older and poorer as the suburb attracts its younger families and grows "fat" on their incomes.

This *de facto* segregation is accompanied by block busting tactics in many urban communities. Community segregation leads to segregation in schools, followed by the inevitable decline in educational funds and standards. The resultant urban ghettos seethe with hostility as they perpetuate the low self-image of their population. To facilitate the suburbanite's transportation problems, freeways are constructed through the city and disrupt its neighborhoods and pollute its environment. Attempts to penetrate these discriminating structures with programs for metropolitan school busing or suburban low cost housing have met with strong resistance. Yet no alternative programs that would involve the suburbanite in urban responsibility have been proposed.

All societal structures together with the cultural values that sustain them are products of human beings. Consequently they do not qualify as objects for human worship. All societies, including the community in which you live, are in varying degrees less than the kingdom of God. Therefore they need to be constantly scrutinized. It is to this task that God's people are especially called.

Chapter 4

The Priest and the Prophet
in the Old Testament

The two ways of caring—care for the individual person, marriage, family, and care for the corporate structures of society—can be compared to the roles of priest and prophet in the Old Testament. These terms bring differing images to our minds. We think of a priest, therefore, as someone who functions before an altar in a church. Or the idea of hearing confessions may come to mind. Another image is that of intercessor or mediator. Often the priest is pictured in elaborate garb performing sacred ritual. My use of the terms is concerned more with the kind of caring the priest performed rather than with his various ways of performing it. The priest is a mediator of healing and reconciliation. He may perform this function as a leader of worship, or as a preacher, or as a pastoral counselor, or as an understanding person in an unstructured conversation.

The images of the prophet are even more varied than that of the priest. For most people a prophet is one who foretells the future. For some he is an ecstatic who utters in some mysterious way divine oracles. In the New Testament, prophecy was considered a special gift of the Spirit. My use of the term concerns the focus of the prophet's message rather than the manner in which it was delivered. The word *prophet* means to "speak for" and the prophet of the Lord spoke for the Lord. His message concerned the behavior of his people. He spoke for God concerning the injustices and idolatries that corrupted his society. It was on the basis of these moral and spiritual conditions that he made many of his predictions concerning the future.

The Priest as Leader in Worship Life

The priest was the leader in the worship life of the people of Israel. A major function of his vocation was that of offering sacrifices as a mediator between God and his people. These sacrifices were of livestock or grain. The first fruits offerings and the free will offerings of substance were usually of grain, while sacrifices for sins were of animals.

The blood of the animal was the expression of its life. In shedding its blood the priest mediated for the sinner. The sacrifice was a symbolic act indicating the gravity of sin. The procedure with its detailed ritual symbolically expressed both the movement of the sinner toward God and the movement of God toward the sinner. Although some sins were considered too serious for expiation through sacrifice, the observation of the New Testament writer of the Letter to the Hebrews is still an apt observation of mediation under the Old Covenant: "without the shedding of blood there is no forgiveness of sins" (Heb. 9:22).

The sin offerings had their culmination in the annual Day of Atonement. According to the prescribed ritual for this day the high priest alone entered the inner court of the temple, the holy of holies, where he offered a sacrifice for his own sins and the sins of the community. An additional animal, the scapegoat, was driven into the wilderness to die after the high priest had symbolically placed upon it the sins of the people. Although this practice has long been discarded, the psychological need for such a transference of guilt remains. The psychological scapegoat, however, is a human being instead of an animal. Also, instead of reserving the practice for a yearly ritual, it is a familiar feature of our social and family structures.

The Prophet as Cultural Critic

There were various kinds of prophets in the Old Testament and not all had the same emphasis. The prophet was considered a sacred person by the people, one possessed by the Spirit of God, and wore the identifying prophet's mantle. Some prophets were associated with the temple, although unofficially, while others functioned outside the temple. Some were solitary figures like Elijah while others were in companies, often called sons of the prophets, like Elisha. The canonical prophets—those whose writings appear in the Old Testament are known for their denunciations of the injustices in Israelite society. They espoused the cause of the oppressed and called for the repentance of those who contributed, directly or indirectly, by commission or omission, to such exploitation.

The prophet and priest were complementary in their roles in Israel. In actual practice, however, they were also at times antagonistic to each other. Dismayed by the lack of penitence of some for whom the priest was offering sacrifice, the prophet reacted vehemently. Some of his denunciations sound as though he was against sacrifices in themselves. Naturally this upset the priest. Such prophets, he charged, were meddling in other people's business.

"What to me is the multitude of your sacrifices? says the Lord; I have had enough of burnt offerings of rams and the fat of fed beasts; I do not delight in the blood of bulls, or of lambs, or of he-goats" (Isa. 1:11). These words of Isaiah echoed those of the earlier prophet Amos. "Even though you offer me your burnt offerings and cereal offerings, I will not accept them, and the peace offerings of your fatted beasts I will not look upon . . . but let justice roll down like waters and righteousness like an everflowing stream" (Amos 5:22-24).

Statements such as these got Amos in trouble with Amaziah the priest of Bethel who reported him as a subversive to the King. "Amos," he said, "has conspired against you in the midst of the house of Israel: the land is not able to bear all his words" (Amos 7:10). Jeremiah also experienced the ire of the priests. On one occasion he was physically beaten by Pashur the priest and put in stocks in the temple (Jer. 20:1-2). For a time he was forbidden even to enter the temple (Jer. 36:5). The antagonism was mutual. "Thus says the Lord of hosts, the God of Israel," the prophet charged. "Add your burnt offerings to your sacrifices, and eat the flesh, for in the day that I brought them out of the land of Egypt I did not speak to your fathers or command them concerning burnt offerings and sacrifices. But this command I gave them. Obey my voice . . ." (Jer. 7:21-23).

Jesus used a quotation from the prophet Hosea on two occasions in his conflict with the Pharisees over the spirit and the letter of the law: "I desire mercy and not sacrifice" (Hos. 6:6; cf. Matt. 9:13; 12:7). Yet he also encouraged people to offer sacrifices. The various lepers whom he had healed for example, were directed to go to the priest to offer the prescribed sacrifices for cleansing. (Luke 5:14, Mark 1:44, Matt. 8:4, Lev. 14:1-32) What he and the prophets before him were attacking was not the offering of sacrifice as such but the separation of the act of sacrifice from the thoughts and intents of the heart. It was to prevent this misuse that Jesus and the prophets attacked the priestly sacrifice. In the ministry of Jesus the prophetic and the priestly roles are united: he was a prophet after the likeness of Moses (Acts 3:22) and also a priest after the order of Melchizedek (Heb. 6:20).

Different Basis for Vocation

The priest became a priest in a way radically different from the way a prophet became a prophet. The priest inherited his position. The tribe of Levi was chosen as the priestly tribe. Instead of having their allotment of land like the other tribes, the Levites were dispersed throughout the tribes. The high priest was selected from the Levitical family of Aaron, the brother of Moses. In contrast the prophet had a personal or individual sense of call, or compulsion, to be God's spokesman. There seems to have been some loose institutionalization among the sons of the prophets and the so-called cultic prophets associated with the temple. Some scholars believe the latter had a definite function in the liturgy of the temple services. The distinguishing feature of a prophet, however, was that he believed himself to be possessed by the Spirit of God.

The prophet's call was at times against his own desires. The story of Jonah and the big fish is the familiar example of a reluctant prophet. After his unsuccessful attempt to run away from his distasteful call to preach to the people of

Nineveh, Jonah finally fulfilled his assignment, but hated every minute of it. Nor was he the only prophet to hate his message. Jeremiah was called to the task of warning his people that God would not protect them against the Babylonians. Therefore he advocated early appeasement. This put him under the unenviable suspicion of being a traitor. Anguishing over his miserable lot the prophet pleaded with God to relieve him of the assignment, but to no avail. "If I say, 'I will not mention him, or speak any more in his name,' there is in my heart as it were a burning fire shut up in my bones, and I am weary with holding it in, and I cannot" (Jer. 20:9).

When the prophet said, "Thus says the Lord," his message went beyond any personal or political considerations. He was God's spokesman. Since the source of his message and the basis for his authority lay outside the established institutions of his society, he was in a freer position to oppose these institutions than if he were obligated to them, even the institution of the Levitical priesthood.

Priest and Prophet in the Political Process

As an institution of power in Israelite society the priests also were involved in political issues. At times this involvement meant martyrdom. When Ahimelech the priest gave hospitality to David and his men in their flight from King Saul, he was endangering his own security. Betrayed by an informer he and eighty-five priests were executed by Saul for this act. In contrast to the prophet, however, the priest's political involvement as illustrated by Ahimelech was more one of loyalty to those he considered rightfully claimants to the throne than that of a cultural critic.

Although a prophet could not become a priest unless he

was a Levite, a priest could become a prophet. The prophet Ezekiel, for example, was also a priest. Perhaps it is significant that he functioned as a prophet in Babylon with a captive people where Israel's social and political institutions were uprooted.

The prophet's inner direction as one possessed by the Spirit of God made him an unpredictable political ally; he might as easily become a critic. Although the prophet Isaiah functioned as somewhat of a court chaplain, the government could not thereby assume his support. When King Hezekiah became overly elated by the attention of envoys from Babylon, he showed them his treasure house. Apparently aware of this event, Isaiah queried Hezekiah about it. When told that the envoys had been shown everything in the storehouse Isaiah said, "Hear the word of the Lord of hosts. Behold the days are coming when all that is in your house and that which your fathers have stored up till this day, shall be carried into Babylon; nothing shall be left" (Isa. 38:5-6).

Conflict with the False Prophet

On this question of support for the sovereign the true prophets had their conflict with the false prophets. Although this differentiation of true and false was made by those whom we call the true prophets, there is nevertheless some element of objectivity in their distinction. Jeremiah lamented to God that those who were making his distasteful task all the more distasteful were those who called themselves prophets of God. "Ah Lord God, behold, the prophets say to them, 'You shall not see the sword, nor shall you have famine, but I will give you assured peace in this place' " (Jer. 14:13). He was predicting doom and they, deliverance—all in the name of the same God. No prophet of God can promise *assured*

41

peace to any human community. As Reinhold Niebuhr has pointed out, this kind of prophecy is false because it assures the sinner peace and security within the terms of his sinful ambitions: peace in his sins rather than through the forgiveness of sins *(Beyond Tragedy.* New York: Chas. Scribner's Sons 1937, p. 95).

These false prophets may have been simply feathering their nests by ingratiating themselves with the prevailing power structure. On the other hand, they may have been sincere. In this case they had become acculturated. Identifying the society of Israel with the kingdom of God, they were insensitive to the discrepancies between the two.

The conflict of the true prophets with the false prophets is similar to the prophet's conflict with the priests. While the priests in question were not necessarily proclaiming "assured peace in this place," they were saying the same in effect by the way they were conducting their office. Although they acknowledged the reality of sin "in this place," they were offering sacrifices for forgiveness as a formality rather than as a means for change. Their ritual by-passed repentance. Despite this possible distinction from the false prophet, Jeremiah lumps both priest and prophet together in this denunciation: "Both prophet and priest are ungodly; even in my house I have found their wickedness, says the Lord" (Jer. 23:11).

The prophet's conflict with priest and false prophet concerned their relationship to the established institutions of society. The false prophet and the loyal priests were rewarded; their position in society was secure. In contrast we find the prophet Micaiah in King Ahab's dungeon for refusing God's blessing on the king of Israel's plan to unite with the king of Judah in an attack on the king of Syria. When the attendant from Ahab summoned Micaiah from the dungeon for another opportunity to speak favorably to the king, he said, "Behold the words of the prophets with one accord are favorable to the king: let your word be like the word of one of them and speak favorably" (1 Kings 22:13). Despite this pressure Micaiah again proclaimed the opposite; the king was furious and returned him to the dungeon. The same thing happened later to Jeremiah. He had refused repeatedly to tell King Zedekiah what he wanted to hear regarding his policy toward Babylon. As a result he remained in Zedekiah's dungeon. Meanwhile the false prophets enjoyed the king's favor by saying the words he wanted to hear.

The "Kept" Problem

The problem of the "kept" prophet or the "kept" priest is chronic to all societies including our own. Those covenanted to God are still obligated to the "hand that feeds them," or befriends them. How then can one be free to exercise a prophetic role when his word from the Lord may be contrary to what these significant others want to hear?

Following the Attica Prison revolt syndicated newspaper columnist Garry Wills asked, "Where Were the Chaplains?" Why, he asked, are the people whom we would expect to be the voices for prison reform silent? "Chaplaincies as a whole are mere instruments of assuagement," he wrote. "They try to oil the works with prayer, make things run smoother. Their function is life-adjustment, and what they adjust to is the institution's needs." The same criticism has been aimed at the armed services chaplain whose voice had been conspicuously silent in regard to the Vietnam war protest.

Prison chaplains and military chaplains are in potentially compromising positions. Their opportunities, often their salary, and certainly their tenure, are under the control of the institutions toward which they could exercise a prophetic function. The service chaplain needs the cooperation of the "old man" if he is to conduct an effective ministry with his men. Consequently he feels the pressure to curry his favor. Yet who of us, clergyman or layman, is not compromised— "kept"—to some extent, in some ways, by some phase of "the system?" How free are we in our respective positions in society to function as mouthpieces for God? As Wills put it, "If even our prophets are slaves, what must the rest of us be?"

The slogan, "America, Love It or Leave It" expresses a kind of institutional loyalty that precludes criticism. It is clearly not the kind of loyalty toward the state that characterized the canonical prophets of Israel.

In spite of their recurring antagonisms the priestly emphasis and the prophetic emphasis are essentially complementary. Either one alone tends to become distorted. The priestly emphasis on the needs of the individual without the balance of the prophetic emphasis on the needs of society leads to an attitude of adjustment to the ills of society. The priestly emphasis apart from the prophetic encourages one to concentrate on himself. He is challenged to shape up to what *is*. In so doing he is abetting the status quo in his social environment. As the imbalance increases, the religious experience of the individual, the comfortable feelings of the counselee, or the "assured peace" of the devotee to ecclesiastical ritual assume primacy over moral behavior.

On the other hand the prophetic emphasis apart from the priestly emphasis leads to utopian illusions about building the kingdom of God on earth. Overlooking the evil in every good and in every person, including the person of the prophet, the unbalanced prophetic emphasis develops a falsely sim-

44

plistic solution to social problems. "Our own flesh" is projected into the world where it becomes identified with a specific social evil or a particular privileged group. Even if the necessary changes take place in the structures of society, evil, like a trojan horse, would enter into the new order through its citizens. The potential for corruption can be lessened but not eliminated by changes in the structures.

Need for Complementation

The priestly and the prophetic emphases worked together in Old Testament times even though occasionally there were bitter antagonisms. So also in our day the complement of the two is needed. The prophet's call for repentance is in effect a call for the priest's reconciling ministry, but at the level of spirit rather than form. Yet forms are necessary for the spirit to express itself. Although they are indispensable, forms can become the victims of age and routine and become separated from their original spirit. "Time makes ancient goods uncouth." When this happens we search for new forms or seek to revitalize the old ones. Contemporary worship services with their openness to imagination and innovation are an example of this search for new forms to express the spirit. So also is the growing emphasis on small groups within the congregation in which persons are encouraged to share their concerns honestly. Through these new media the old gospel of reconciliation is freshly experienced.

Repentance means a change of mind, of direction, of life style. It is initiated by contrition and culminated by behavioral change. Repentance is possible because reconciliation is a reality. How can one take a good hard look at himself unless he knows that there is nothing in what he may see that can

45

disqualify him from the love of God? The good news of reconciliation is that nothing in all creation can separate us from the love of God in Christ Jesus (Rom. 8:37). The assurance of reconciliation frees us up to make changes in our lives.

Chapter 5

The Contemporary Priest and Prophet

Although the priest and the prophet complement one another in the Israelite culture and provide us with an illustration of the church's continuing need for this balance in its forms of care, the terms themselves need to be declericalized. Priest and prophet convey an implicit professionalism; in short, they sound like terms for the clergy. The ministry of the laity has been consistently overshadowed by that of the clergy and there is no point in reenforcing this discrimination. In fact, the challenge is to remove it.

The Use of Uniforms to Differentiate

The minimization of the laity in the church's ministry has been accentuated by the use of uniforms to identify the clergy. In our day as in Israel the priests wear vestments. Since the liturgical renewal in our recent past some denominations have experienced an increased elaboration in these vestments. Only in the most informal of Protestant groups do the clergy still wear "street clothes" when officiating in Sunday morning worship. What were considered "far out" vestments worn only by the more "liturgically minded" clergy when I graduated from a theological seminary, are now not only generally accepted in my own denomination but also by groups considered less formal. Uniforms in themselves do not create differences in status; only attitudes can do this. Uniforms, however, make whatever differentiation that is present, highly visible.

The contemporary analog to the prophet's mantle is the clerical collar. Like the mantle it is worn outside the sanctuary as well as inside. Therefore it is even more conspicuous to the general public than the priestly vestments. The news media notes the presence of the church at any occasion by this uniform, and also by the garb of the female religious. This has led to the practice of wearing the collar in public demonstrations. Even clergymen of denominations who historically have protested against any identifying garb for clergy are now wearing it to make such an identification.

There has been a justified antagonism toward such attempts visibly to identify the church's presence. Most of these have come from lay people who resent having their clergy taking such deliberately visible stands in their identification as the church. Naturally this antagonism is most likely to occur when the lay person in question disagrees with the stand that is being taken. Despite the prejudiced nature of his objection, he still has a legitimate complaint. When clergymen utilize a uniform purposefully to represent the church in public affairs, particularly those of a controversial nature, they leave the lay person very unidentified in any public sense with this same church. Because the lay person is not recognized, he or she is not reckoned as the church, not only when absent, but even when present.

Waste of Lay Power

The result of this clericalizing of the church is a tragic waste of lay power. Robert Hudnut calls the church *The Sleeping Giant* because it has tremendous potential in its lay people to influence one another and all of society. Its sleeping condition is the non-actualization of this potential.

This power is priestly as well as prophetic. The lay person is uniquely equipped through his own experience and through his personal contacts to care for those who are in straits similar to those he has known. This priestly potential, of course, is being actualized in unorganized ways. The loss occurs in its lack of organization within the structures of the institutional church.

A well known example of lay priestly power is Alcoholics Anonymous. It is significant that while AA originated outside the organized church, in spite of the need for it within the church, its orientation and practice are implicitly Christian. Its therapeutic foundation is the grace of God. Realizing he is defeated the alcoholic surrenders himself to the Higher Power, whom he believes will accept him as he is—a defeated alcoholic. There is mutual confession, sharing, and caring in the AA group and the fifth step in the program is a rigorous exercise in the priestly confessional.

There are also instances of lay priestly caring in the organized efforts of local congregations. One church with which I am familiar has a grief therapy program in which those in the congregation who have experienced bereavement meet regularly for training in the caring for the bereaved. When the pastor has a funeral, a lay grief therapist is assigned to the family of the deceased. Among other services he makes a pledge to visit the bereaved regularly for one year. This same congregation has a weekly psychodrama under qualified lay leadership where people can act out their needs and receive enlightenment and support. Beside the person whose problem is being dramatized, others in the group are directed to take the roles of the significant people in his life. A priestly ministry of caring takes place as traumatic situations are reenacted and discussed. (For a description of this ministry see *Group Counseling in the Church,* by John Oman, Augsburg, 1972.)

Another congregation has organized a group of men to call regularly on men in the community penal institutions and to assist them when they are released. There are many other examples of organized priestly activity in congregations. Yet the unlimited potential can be developed further in actions of priestly care in marriage crises, parent-youth gaps, vocation-employment problems, and other specialized needs.

The sleeping giant is sleeping also in its prophetic potential. Lay people's opportunities through their various vocations to exercise an influence for social justice is again unlimited. The legal profession in particular has recently challenged young attorneys with prophetic vision. Ralph Nader's raiders are the most familiar example of this challenge. Other lesser known but equally effective legal minds are also working for better laws and better enforcement of existing laws to insure social justice, pollution control, and consumer protection.

Yet the legal profession is only one among many vocations of power in our society. In smaller communities church members may occupy most or even all of the decision making positions affecting the life of the community. On one occasion when I was discussing the prophetic way of caring with the council of an influential church in a small community, the chairman made the rather awesome observation that virtually every elected position in the community was held by a member of that church!

Despite this prophetic potential in its own midst local congregations as a whole have not nurtured, educated, or even supported these potential prophets in their ministry. Instead they have developed an institutionalized conception of church work that has no connection with the vocational opportunities of its members. A layman prominent in the educational world of our community was asked to participate in a panel concerning the church's role in urban problems. Speaking directly to the assembly clergy he said, "I have been in education for twenty years and during this time I have had many frustrations as well as opportunities in seeking to improve the lot of minority groups in education. Also during this time I have belonged to three different churches. Yet at no time did I receive any specific support or guidance from my church for my vocational challenge. Instead I was given an usher button as a fulfillment of my service obligation to the church."

Families That Are Hurting

The Christian conception of vocation includes also our responsibilities in family living. The record of churches in assisting people in this vocation is only a little better than it is in regard to their community vocations. The most familiar family education programs are secularly oriented. Therefore many church members do not see the connection of these programs with the church's mission. Consequently programs such as Parent Effectiveness Training, the Family Education Centers of the Alfred Adler Institute, or even Transactional Analysis—like Alcoholics Anonymous—are potential replacements for the church.

In a newspaper feature concerning the Alfred Adler Institute the reporter interviewed a family consisting of father, mother, and four children. After a traumatic mother-daughter clash the family had sought assistance from an Alderian Family Education Center. The result after sixteen months was a changed family. "We were just floundering around before," said the mother. "It's pulled our family together." Besides attending the weekly counseling sessions at the center, the family is also assisting as counselors at the session. "In a way," said the mother, "it has become for us what the church used to be" (*Minneapolis Tribune,* Feb. 27, 1972).

She could scarcely have said this if their church had been a help to them in their family problems. Many families today are hurting badly because of the changes in society that have widened the generation (or communication) gap. Mothers and fathers—as well as their children—desperately need help in coping with their problems. Parents are confused and upset over what they should say and how they should act in a day when the old assumptions regarding child rearing have been challenged. They are looking to their church for help in these concerns. But churches like other societal institutions have been slow to face up to changes. Parent Effectiveness Education, Transactional Analysis, and the Adlerian Institutes are popular because they relate to a great need. But where does this leave the church? One mother put it succinctly even if bitterly: "My faith has offered me much in my despair but my church has offered me nothing."

Some churches are utilizing these popular methodologies in their own counseling and educational ministries. This, of course, is a help in connecting the church's mission with family life. However, unless the people of the church understand that their function in family responsibilities is a Christian vocation and therefore a service of the church, they may interpret the church's utilization of these programs as simply a new way to "get with it." This understanding is also a protection for these methodologies. As good and helpful as they are, none is another gospel. They can be valuable approaches to problems for those who believe the gospel. They are undoubtedly helpful for those also who do not believe. But they will not prove ultimately helpful to those who try to get from them more than they are meant to give.

The Need for Organization

Prophetic power is also people power. Citizens' groups have rediscovered this power in our day of social activism. Exerting pressure simply by the number and visibility of their physical bodies, loosely organized groups have been successfully influencing the power structures of society. The church has people. As a corporate body these people are a potential for effecting change simply by their numbers. If a sufficient number of people in a congregation, or better, in several local congregations, can agree concerning their specific responsibilities to their society—and this is a big *if*—they can exercise their people-power in fulfilling those responsibilities. This power is rarely used. Although there are a number of reasons for this neglect, one in particular is the identification of the church with the clergy. In comparison to the laity, the number of clergy is insignificant.

To actualize this potential of layman in both priestly and prophetic dimensions, considerable effort needs to be given to the task of organization. Otherwise those who are hurting and those who could care for them in these hurts may pass each other as the proverbial ships in the night. Here the clergyman is needed. Hopefully he (or she) has been educated for this responsibility. He is also paid by the congregation to perform it. As the catalyst for lay ministry he is called by the laity not only to care for them but also to equip them to care for one another and for the community. He is set aside—ordained—by the people of God for this purpose. Sometimes, however, it is easier and more ego inflating to be the indispensable minister than the catalyst for ministry. Instead of the development of lay power, there is the sad and repeated history of clergy usurpation of lay responsibility. Nor is this all the fault of the clergyman; laymen have encouraged the usurpation. It is tempting to pay someone to fulfill your obligations. Society also is a conspirator; it prefers to consider the clergy as a special breed rather than as organizers within a special breed.

George W. Webber defines the clergyman's function as that of community organizer. The frequent complaint is that the pastor is too involved in the community. When he fulfills his calling as community organizer, this complaint will no longer be heard. Instead of the pastor being the minister for the congregation to the community, the laity will be involved in this capacity.

Even the organizing role is not exclusively that of the clergy. In my community, for example, a lay woman has taken the initiative to organize local congregations in a prophetic way of caring. Each congregation has representatives to the working group which meets regularly to ascertain the community needs and to act concertedly to meet them. The group is called C.O.M.E.—Congregations on the Move for Equality. They supply emergency food and clothing to destitute families or persons who for one reason or another cannot receive it at the moment from the welfare agencies. They have worked politically to influence suburban village councils to approve low cost federal housing. They have worked for racial equality by exerting pressure on mail order houses to employ black models for their catalogs and have even sponsored training programs to prepare them. In addition they publish a monthly news letter which draws attention to national and local issues pertinent to a prophetic ministry.

Appropriate Lay Categories

Although we have permitted them to become professionalized, the categories of priest and prophet are old and familiar terms in our ecclesiastical tradition for specific functions in which the distinction between lay or clergy is immaterial. The priest as a professional, called and ordained, is dependent on the priesthood of all believers. Before his ordination set him apart, the clergyman had already been set apart. He was baptized into the communion of saints. The word saint means one who is set apart for God. The lay person is no less a saint than the clergy and therefore no less apart—no less a priest. Ordination is an act of the people of God—the company of priests. It is the whole people of God who participate in the healing power of the gospel and who minister the same to one another.

Based on the calling of God to all vocations, the prophetic way of caring is carried out through lay involvement as a leaven in society (Luke 13:21). The clergyman prophet is too limited by his profession to function alone. It is the lay people who occupy the positions of power in the various sectors of society. The complement to the priesthood of all believers is the prophethood of all believers. God's spokesmen are already strategically placed.

The church and its ministry are predominately lay. This is obvious in terms of numbers and potential influence. It is also intuitively obvious to lay people whose religion is a basic influence in their lives. In some congregations, such as those described by Robert Coles in his study, *God and the Rural Poor,* lay people may conceive of the church as theirs rather

55

than the pastor's. The rural poor as Coles describes them gather in their churches to minister to one another as priests. Through this experience they receive the strength to carry on in the face of their privation and suffering. The preacher who did not share the poverty may have been lacking also in empathy *(Psychology Today,* Jan. 1972, p. 35).

While the priestly function of the church centering in the fellowship of believers sustained the rural poor—black and white—in the midst of hopeless poverty, their prophetic function was lacking. The support they received from their church helped them to endure but not to protest. With the beginning of the civil rights movement many black churches have changed. While still offering comfort and strength to the suffering, they have also become involved in changing the societal cause for much of this suffering.

Naturally this has changed their "image." Those who opposed the changes in society that the black church was seeking were offended. Agitation of this sort is not the church's business! So black churches were bombed. To the outraged attackers these buildings could no longer be considered churches. Only when they are confined in their functions to the priestly dimensions are they churches. Prophets were stoned in Israel. Prophetic churches have their sanctuaries bombed in the United States.

It is one thing to unite those who are hurting to seek to change their oppressive environment; it is another to unite those who are not hurting to effect such changes. This is the obstacle to the prophetic way of caring among the so-called white churches, most of whom are composed of people profiting from the status quo. Instead of exerting corporate pressure on the power structures to make room for them, the people of our white churches must exert pressure on their own structures—on themselves—to share their power and privileges with others. While admittedly a tougher job, it is also more specifically Christian. In the New Testament Christians are encouraged to seek the good of the neighbor rather than their own (1 Cor. 10:24).

Obviously this is not the way we expect human beings to function. The best we can hope for, it seems, is an enlightened self-interest. History provides many examples of the poor banding together, whether Christian or not, to exert pressure for change, but examples of the affluent banding together, even in Christ's name, to share some of their privileges with others, have been rare. Instead we have lonely individuals, prophets, who call for sacrifice, and unusual individuals who respond.

Chapter 6

The Church's Golden Age in Retrospect

The church in America reached its greatest popularity in the nineteen fifties and early sixties. Like most good old days this period probably had more conflicts and contradictions than we now recall. In retrospect, however, it was the golden age.

There is more than retrospect to substantiate the heights of this period; our statistics and polls are on record as testimony. Church attendance climbed to an all-time high. So did church membership. The same was true of the church's popularity. Where now it is most frequently referred to negatively in terms of its failures and deficiencies, the church then was frequently commended for its contributions to society. Evidently sufficient numbers of those who had turned to it for solace and hope during the dark days of World War II felt satisfied with its care. It was during this war that there were "no atheists in the foxholes." The times were right for the churches and they enjoyed the public's good will.

Realizing their opportunities the churches were quick to

respond. As tangible institutions they expanded greatly. Denominational home missions departments had a field day. My own church body established as many as one hundred and eighty new churches in one year as compared to twenty-two for 1971. Nearly all of these in the golden age were in the new burgeoning suburbs.

Characterized by Activity

Congregational life was characterized by much activity. In fact the term "active congregation" was the choice accolade. The activity centered in many organizations and committees. The pastor served as a sort of executive secretary, making sure that these organizations and committees were all active and hopefully coordinating their efforts.

During the golden age there were also many church building programs. Churches that were not relocating in the growing suburbs were adding parish halls or educational units. All of this consumed huge amounts of the energy of pastors and lay people. It also consumed a major portion of the congregation's financial outlay. In expanding its facilities a congregation was providing tangible evidence of its activity and of its progress.

In the meantime, however, the trends were being initiated that would threaten to destroy the cities. Even as the suburbs have prospered, so also have the suburban churches, but each at the expense of the city and its remaining churches. Now it is the diaspora in the suburbs who take up offerings for the poor in the old city from which they have come.

As we might anticipate, the close of the golden age is noted by the rise of its critics. In an article with a golden age title, "The Crowded Temple," Loren Halvorson reflected on all the activity: "Though it has been delightful to have basked in the organizational affluence of the church and to have been intoxicated with the visions of the church in full fortissimo, this has, nevertheless, all been very exhausting." *(Dialog,* Winter 1962, p. 31). Two titles of books during this period express their indictments: *The Suburban Captivity of the Churches* by Gibson Winter and *The Noise of Solemn Assemblies* by Peter Berger. Winter, a theological professor, attacked the activity syndrome of the suburban churches as trivial and irrelevant and concluded that such exhausting drudgery must be the golden age's way of atoning for its guilt. Sociologist Berger, as his title indicates, attacked the parochial nature of the church's activity and concluded that the essential tasks of the church's mission must be undertaken outside the local congregation. To show that the golden age was not confined to American churches, Canadian Pierre Berton published a similar critique with a similar title, *The Comfortable Pew.*

These critiques as well as others accuse the church of becoming institutionally inverted. Enamored by its highly organized religious fellowship the local congregation too often confined its mission to its institutionally oriented programs. As a result the prophetic way of caring tended to become even more dormant than it had been.

A Comfortable Adustment

With the continuing decline of the prophetic emphasis and the rise of material affluence, the people of the white churches tended to accept whatever was comfortable in their social environs rather than what was just. In their minds the values of the surrounding culture and the values of the Christian faith were becoming increasingly indistinguishable. Because they were functioning well within the structures of society they uncritically assumed these structures were adequate for all.

The church as an institution was functioning equally well. Occasional tensions in the adjustment were pushed to the periphery. There was just too much going on to give them much attention. Things were not all as they should be, obviously, but life was certainly better in the "righteous empire" than anywhere else! Besides people weren't ready for societal changes, we said, and it was not considered wise to disrupt our well functioning institutions just to hurry the process.

As a young pastor in these days I took an interest in a newly organized congregation in the black section of town and thought it a good gesture to share pulpits with the black pastor. When I mentioned the idea to the church council, I was kindly but firmly advised to forget it. Some people wouldn't like it, I was told. So I dropped it. Besides I was concerned about other problems. The local theater was hosting a Eugene O'Neill play with all the bad words. Although I hadn't seen it, I wrote a letter of protest to the local paper. The fall festival of the local Catholic Church had beer and bingo contrary to the local community ordinance. That was worth another letter. While not everyone in the congregation may have agreed with my stands on these matters, I received no criticism since these positions were in the traditional stance of individual morality of the American Protestant tradition.

In spite of this tendency to be preoccupied with trivia, the church in the golden age offered a helpful ministry to many people. The priestly caring of pastoral counseling became popular during this time. It was a caring, however, that was performed almost exclusively by the clergy. Many who were suffering from anxiety and depression responded to the invitation to seek counsel from the pastor. People with marital problems increasingly looked to the pastoral counselor for help. I wrote a book for pastors during this period entitled *How to Start Counseling.* A pastor who was swamped by his counseling load quipped I should write a sequel entitled, *How to Stop Counseling.*

The ministry offered by the churches had a strong family orientation. Church going itself was prompted as a wholesome family activity. "Church Going Families are Happier Families," appeared even on community billboards. While the highly developed program of the congregation might seem to have taken people away from their families, they were in a sense still in a family activity, since there was an organization for each family member. This potential divisiveness, however, was often discussed and one congregation of my acquaintance decided to hold all of its organizational meetings on the same evening so that the family could at least come together and also return together.

Primarily one of spiritual comfort and inner peace, the gospel of the golden age also had its obligations. Beside the expected standards for personal morality, these obligations related to a regular participation in the congregation's activities. A paragraph that I wrote for our weekly parish paper regarding the approaching new year together with its heading clearly shows the emphasis.

Read Before the Hour of the New Year

Next Sunday is January 2. What better way can we begin the New Year than by all of us attending worship. Something very important is missing from your week when you miss church. We feel better mentally, physically, and spiritually for having been to church. It is the spiritual tonic that makes the week go so much better in every way. Your personal, marital, and family happiness is greatly increased by your regular church attendance.

Though it demanded loyalty to its program the church of the golden age resisted putting its own particular cultural values under the judgment of the cross of Christ. This cross exposes the evil in the good, the sham in the religious act, and the corruption in the structures of power. Jesus fulfilled the prophetic function and exposed the evils in Israelite society. The cross was his "reward." Under its judgment our culture's standards for success risk being revealed as failure. Since the churches had adopted some of these standards to measure the success of their own institutions, they were understandably reluctant to risk the judgment. Such reluctance only entrenched their acculteration. The Christian faith had to conform to the cultural values. The process can take place with such rationalization that one is only mildly aware of any points of tension. It can happen in this way when the voice of the prophet is dim.

In its adaptability the church in this era was simply reflecting a general societal apathy toward social issues. Youth, the great protestors of our day, were silent. During the middle fifties a national magazine had a feature report on youth's lack of drive, including students. The Korean War was over and the young veterans were happy to be home. They and others like them were looking for a period of respite. Instead of wanting to climb to the top of the hill, the report stated, students were content with a niche in the side. Security was uppermost and the middle of the road looked like the best place to find it. But as has been observed, you don't straighten a tipped boat by sitting in the middle. Rather you contribute to the problem.

Christians, like others, too often reflect their own particular cultural environment rather than functioning as a leaven or a conscience within it. They realize how difficult it is to assert themselves in the presence of those who hold conflicting opinions.

Need for Prophetic Ministry

During the golden age we needed more prophets like Amos, who would speak at the critical moment for God. "Take away from me the noise of your songs, to the melody of your harps I will not listen. But let justice roll down like waters and righteousness like an everflowing stream" (Amos 5:23-24). Take the plight of our cities, for example. There were some protests against abandoning the city even in the golden age, but they were weak and ineffective.

Even among those who stayed there was little interest in ministering to the community in either a priestly or prophetic way. At a recent conference on the plight of the churches still remaining in a large midwestern city the question was raised whether there would be any congregations of that denomination left in that city by the next decade. The few struggling churches that remain are faced with the possible choice of moving out or dying out.

There is, of course, another alternative. The wealthier churches of the area in suburbs, small towns, and rural areas could invest money into the ministry of these hard pressed urban churches to assist them to develop the best possible ways of serving their present communities. But this kind of response requires sacrifice and commitment. While we are reaping the harvest of a previous lack of prophetic vision, there is still time to change our priorities—still time to repent. Happily there are some encouraging examples of such sacrifice and commitment.

The church needs the prophetic ministry for its own welfare. We have been too long under the illusion that because a person believes in Christ he will automatically do the right thing in his vocational responsibilities. Nor can we continue to escape the dilemma by charging one with insincerity in his faith when he acts out of his prejudices to support oppression. The old dictum, "Love God and do as you please," is too simplistic a formula because it overlooks the process of acculturation. Our perception of what is just in any situation is influenced by the kind of social structures with which we are familiar. Rather than testing all things and holding fast to that which is good, as St. Paul suggests, we tend to test only that which is strange to us while that which is familiar is accepted without examination.

Believers need the prophetic ministry to develop their sensitivity to injustice and idolatry. They need the stimulation of contact with others who have different assumptions because of differences in background and culture. There is nothing like the monologue of an in-group to dull one's sensitivities and reinforce his prejudices.

Because they were lacking in such prophetic stimulation, people who are by nature fair minded have nevertheless consistently accepted the racial injustices in our society. Not until black people openly rebelled against these injustices in the civil rights movement of the early sixties did many of these people begin to face what they previously were able to avoid. During the golden age most of the white church people were not very perturbed by the fact that black people were excluded from many jobs. The situation was similar for American Indians and Spanish Americans. We gave tacit approval by our silence to injustices that today we would not tolerate. Were these conditions any less just in 1955 than in the 1970s?

Because they are lacking in prophetic stimulation people

with little psychological need to project their guilt on to others are angry at the behavior of marginal and out-groups with whom they have little contact. At the same time they gloss over the evil in the established institutions of society with whom they identify. Yet it was Jesus who identified with the alienated of society and attacked the evils of the establishment.

God's people who have experienced the power of God for change in their own lives need also to function as change agents in the social context in which they live. They need to do so as individuals who live according to the law of love in their vocations. They need to do so also as participants in corporate action. We are called by God to function as priests and as prophets in our *place*. This is the *place* of our relationships—family and community. It is the *place* of our positions of power—vocational and situational. It is the *place* of our opportunities to join with others to influence the institutions of society.

Chapter 7

The Stewardship of Power

Along with the heavily emphasized stewardships of time, talents, and possessions (money) there is also the little emphasized stewardship of power. The possession of power, like the possession of money (often associated with power) is a familiar source of personal and corporate corruption. A steward is different from a possessor in that he manages what he possesses for another. So in contrast to a stewardship in which we manage our power on behalf of the one from whom it is derived, we are tempted to become lords in the use of power and achieve our satisfaction in exercising it over others.

The Exploitative Use of Power

This penchant for domination has produced the long and tragic history of tyrannies within all units of society from the family to the state. There are the familiar political dictatorships maintained by a show of force and the equally familiar power plays executed within families by a more subtle coercion of guilt and fear. Still another form of domination is that asserted by those with the talent of persuasion. They may be top salesmen of insurance or powerful evangelists for religion. That which they have in common is the obvious satisfaction they receive in overpowering people with their expertise in persuasion.

The use of power to dominate provides a sense of security that is basically an illusion. When other persons become objects for manipulation rather than for relationship, one's security depends on controlling these others. What happens then if he cannot do it? The accounts are legion of those who have experienced such demises of power.

All power over others has its limits. Should these limits be reached the manipulator in desperation may become openly despotic. He "pulls out all the stops." Such measures may be temporarily successful. On the other hand they may only dispel whatever doubts their victims may have had concerning their need to emancipate themselves. All that they need now is the opportunity.

In contrast are those who as stewards of power find in their exercise of stewardship a source of personal integrity. It is an expression of their commitment to another. Personal integrity is also a source of security. Unlike the security that depends on dominating others, the security of integrity is sufficient in itself. It does not depend on continual reassurance. While stewards are also subject to the temptations of the flesh, their very acceptance of a stewardship role is a deterrent to the arrogance implicit in the attempt to manipulate another.

Difficulty in Accepting Power

Most of us have more power than we think—or would like to think—to exert in the various sectors of our society. From a Christian perspective this power is a trust from God implicit in our vocations and in our potential as individuals to work together with other individuals. Because it frequently offers no ego satisfaction and may even be ego-threatening, we may be reluctant to use this power. Instead we shrug our shoulders in apparent impotence and lament our inability to do anything. It would seem that we are trying hard to convince ourselves that we are helpless. The shrug, "what can you do?" may become more pronounced with the passing of the years. As one grows older he not only has worked out a system of security that he would rather not threaten, but he also has an investment in that system since his future has become too limited to risk new starts. Gestalt psychologist Frederick Perls says we need to translate "I can't" into "I won't."

Most of us are in positions of influence to a lesser or greater degree. When we consider the scope of this influence within the membership of any one local congregation, it can be quite extensive. To what degree are these members exerting this influence, or, more particularly, to what degree are they accepting their stewardship of power? The answer may depend largely on the support each receives from the other. As a fellowship of believers the congregation is by that same token also a fellowship of stewards. Through this fellowship each can supply the support the other needs.

There is also the potential for each of us to join with others in a corporate effort to effect change. This is people power. It depends on the tangible involvement of persons, having the accumulative effect of sheer numbers or bodies. Like other powers it can be used to satisfy the need to exert power over others. It can also be an effective use of the stewardship of power. This power is given us by God, for it is implicit in our disposition to live together in communities. By the very nature of community life persons can accomplish together what they could not do as individuals. Although we may decline to use this power we can scarcely deny that we have it.

The Fear of Conflict

Whenever we use our power we encounter the possibility of conflict. This is one reason why we may be reluctant to use it. The pressure we exert as stewards may create resistance; people may not take to it kindly. Pressure can be threatening and threatened people become frightened and then angry. Their anger is the offensive thrust of their defensive anxiety, and the steward exerting the pressure is its vulnerable target. The conflict engendered by the use of power produces suffering in the lives of individuals and stress within institutions. The eleventh commandment so far as these institutions—including the church—are concerned, is "Thou shalt not rock the boat!" Like these institutions we create, we as persons also shy away from conflict. In our vocations, friendships, and even our acquaintances, we are reluctant to risk a strain.

The challenge to stewards is to accept conflict if it should result from our exercise of power. Conflict is not only negative; it is also a potential positive. Through conflict can come change, movement, growth and paradoxically, deeper unity. The German sociologist Simmel maintains that the purpose of conflict in social units is to achieve a greater unity in these units. To fulfill this purpose, however, conflict needs to be wisely managed. Our phobia over conflict can frustrate its purpose. Instead of deeper unity, we may achieve only polarization. Because of our anxiety, we avoid conflict, and when it cannot be avoided, we lash out in anger.

Conflict is an integral factor in the dynamic nature of life. It is counteractive to the deadening effect of conformity. By overcoming the inertia in life's routines, conflict can lead to change. It is disruptive to complacency and the subtle injustices, unwarranted assumptions, and myopic limitations that accompany it.

There is obviously a risk in incurring conflict. Yet this risk in negative possibilities is not sufficient reason to leave our power unused. To do so would be like the servant in the parable of the talents who gave his talent back to his Lord wrapped in a napkin (Luke 19:11-27). "I was afraid of you," he said, "because you are a severe man." I was afraid—to use it—afraid of the risk—the consequences, and so here it is— I give it back to you just as I receive it—safe and unused.

But the Lord is not satisfied with the explanation. "You knew that I was a severe man . . . why then did you not put my money into the bank, and at my coming I should have collected it with interest?" In other words, the risk is not only in using it but also in not using it. The Lord wants interest on what he has given us and there is only one way this can be done—put it to use! Of course the interest cannot be guaranteed; there are depressions and bank failures as those who can remember the thirties know only too well. There are also failures in communication and defeats in the use of power. The Lord in the parable seems to be saying to all of this—so what! There is risk in every choice, in every decision, in every commitment, but still you must choose, decide, and commit yourself.

For this kind of existence, "God did not give us the spirit of timidity but a spirit of power and love and self-control" (2 Tim. 1:17). The Lord wants the "talent" of power used like the other "talents," even at the risk of loss. It is the risk of abandonment—of losing one's life, in contrast to seeking to save it—to preserve it. "For whoever would save his life will lose it and whoever loses his life for my sake will save it" (Luke 9:24). "For my sake," is the key to the apparent contradiction. It is a stewardship of power, using it for his sake, rather than as possession of power—using it to satisfy our need to control. In this way losing means saving.

Of course one rarely acts from singleness of motive. It is possible also to "sanctify" our lust for power under the delusion of stewardship. Mixed motivations are "par for the course." It is important that we permit ourselves to recognize them. Being a steward does not depend on having pure motives. It depends on being faithful to Christ in our actions. If we are emancipated from the need to be inwardly pure, we can better evaluate any particular course of action in the light of our vocation as stewards.

"Remembering the Poor"

Normally speaking changes in society are brought about not by those who are comfortable with the way things are, but from those who are not. Those who are being hurt by societal structures push for change, not those who are profiting from these structures. This is, of course, what we would naturally anticipate. Those who are profiting from the *status quo* usually resist change and for obvious reasons. When we are comfortable we do not wish to be disturbed. Those who disturb us are irritants and incur our hostility. On the other hand, those who are hurting "seize the moment" to put on the pressure. They are already irritated by their discomfort, and their hostility either openly or covertly is directed toward the comfortable. Any action that promises change is readily considered.

The exception to these natural reactions would hopefully be "God's people." Wherever they are they have been freed at least to some extent from their cultural environment through their involvement in the kingdom of God—people whose citizenship on earth is radically altered by their simultaneous citizenship in heaven. They have an alternate source of stimulation and motivation and security from that which is conditioned to the values of the culture. They have less reason to be defensive when threatened by the loss of cultural supports and therefore are more open to feel with the hurts of others. So it is that the advantaged in society can empathize with the disadvantaged, and in so doing, participate in the compassion of Christ.

The Gospels repeatedly describe Jesus as moved by compassion when confronted with human suffering. "When he saw the crowds, he had compassion for them because they were harrassed and helpless like sheep without a shepherd" (Matt. 9:36). With this same compassion he was moved to heal their sicknesses. He expressed this compassion physically by reaching out to touch the "untouchable" lepers. This same spirit of compassion characterized the ministry also of his apostles. When missionaries Paul and Barnabas shared the experiences of their ministry to the Gentiles with James, Peter and John in Jerusalem, these apostles gave to them the right hand of fellowship, agreeing to a division of labor between them. They added something, however, which Paul thought significant enough to record: "only they would have us remember the poor." To this he commented—"which very thing I was eager to do" (Gal. 2:19).

This compassion for the poor is spelled out in Jesus' parable in which nations are separated for judgment as a shepherd separates his sheep from the goats. The criteria for this judgment are specific ways in which they did—or did not— "remember the poor." After placing the sheep at his right hand but the goats at his left, Jesus as the judge says to those on his right hand,

"Come, O blessed of my Father, inherit the kingdom prepared for you from the foundation of the world; for I was hungry and you gave me food, I was thirsty and you gave me drink, I was a stranger and you welcomed me, I was naked and you clothed me, I was sick and you visited me, I was in prison and you came to me. Then the righteous will answer him, Lord when did we see thee hungry and feed thee, or thirsty and give thee drink? And when did we see thee a stranger and welcome thee or naked and clothe thee? And the King will answer them, 'Truly, I say to you, as you did it to one of the least of these my brethren, you did it to me' " (Matt. 25:34-40).

Remembering the poor means meeting their needs.

It is difficult now to remember the poor when there are so few of them in our congregations or neighborhoods. The separation of the sheep from the goats on the day of judgment seems to be anticipated by the segregation of the poor from the affluent in contemporary American society. As with most segregations, instead of remembering those with whom we no longer "rub shoulders," we have become suspicious and antagonistic. Attempts to penetrate the boundaries that segregate us are met with resistance. The protest of one suburbanite at a public hearing concerning a proposal for federally subsidized low cost housing spoke for millions of like-minded citizens. "Nobody subsidized me and I don't intend to subsidize anybody else!" This would be tantamount to saying in religious terms, "I've never received grace and I have no intention of letting anyone else receive it." Another put his protest in a more bigoted way. "We came out here to get away from those kind of people!" One can almost hear the Pharisee in the temple, "God I thank you that I am not as other men—particularly the poor."

It is difficult also to visit those in prisons when we do not

76

know any of them. The same segregation seems to exist here also. Fifteen percent of the population of the Minneapolis Workhouse is American Indian. Yet Indians constitute only one percent of the population. This disproportion says more about our societal structures than it does about the Indians. In the Roman Empire of the early centuries of Christendom many of those who filled the jails were there because they were Christians. It is erroneous to assume that those in jail are by that very fact more sinful than the people who are not. The disproportionate number of the poor in our jails today is a by-product of our segregated society.

It was not always so. I can recall as a child going with my parents to deliver baskets at Thanksgiving and Christmas to the poor who belonged to our congregation. We remembered the poor because we *knew* them. The way we remembered was structured by the charity syndrome. The exchange between the givers and receivers implicit in charity is now more critically evaluated. Those blessed with material things give to those deprived of material things. The receivers give only their gratitude. Since it is more blessed to give than to receive, the givers were obviously more blessed. It was a poor exchange so far as self-images were concerned. The givers were elevated in their self-esteem by their "generosity," while the receivers were robbed of this esteem by being only receivers. One's self-image is not elevated by continually being the recipient of other peoples' generosity.

Although government welfare programs have taken over much which was formerly the responsibility of the church in remembering the poor, the same unfortunate exchange continues to exist. What was begun in the Great Depression as a financial support program to get people "back on their feet," has become a way of life for many. The system is now a societal institution with the usual proclivity of institutions to seek to perpetuate themselves. To do so, however, the givers must have receivers. In becoming dependent on the system the poor stay poor or grow poorer. But when welfare becomes a way of life the poor are no longer grateful. How or why should one give gratitude to an impersonal giver?

The poor also have more to give than gratitude. There are other values in life than the material. The poor are persons even as are the affluent, and therefore have something of personal value to give. When Paul was taking a collection from the Gentile Christians for the poor in the congregation at Jerusalem, he reminded them that they were merely participating in an exchange. "For if the Gentiles have come to share in their [the Jews] spiritual blessings, they ought also to be of service to them in material blessings" (Rom. 15:27). One gives spiritual blessings and receives material blessings, while the other gives material blessings and receives spiritual blessings. The exchange is balanced for it is an exchange among equals. Paul was encouraging the Gentiles to remember the poor in Jerusalem as equals before God and therefore equals among people. It is an exchange that elevates the self-image of both participants—for both are contributors as well as receivers.

A Different Kind of Remembering

Through the stewardship of power we have the possibility of achieving a different kind of remembering—one that promotes rather than undermines human dignity. In a balance of the priestly and prophetic ways of caring we can do more than meet the immediate needs of the poor. We are, of course, obligated to remember the poor in the priestly way of feeding the hungry, clothing the naked, billeting the stranger, and visiting the sick and the imprisoned. But we are obligated also to alleviate the injustices in our society that contribute to these needs. We should not be content with the dependency of one group in society on another. As stewards of Christ we can use our power to help bring about an interdependency between groups made possible by a greater sharing of power.

As stewards we are administering for Another. This awareness is an encouragement to humility. It helps to be open to receive from those to whom we are also giving. Our remembering—our giving—is then an experience in mutual respect in which each is before God as the other.

Chapter 8

The Balance in Action

Both priestly and prophetic ways of caring are essential to the church of Jesus Christ and belong together. Care for the individual and care for the social order provide a balance in which each supports the other. Our purpose now is to observe this principle of balance in action.

Priest and Prophet Together

In contrast to the Old Testament patterns from which we developed our categories neither a special calling nor an inherited obligation determine the contemporary functions of prophet and priest. Nor does the rite of ordination. Lay persons are as much involved in these functions as are the clergy. The determinative factor is our belief in Jesus Christ. It is this that provides the calling. Our life with Christ and his people supply the potential to fulfill it.

Some of us are more inclined by background or personality predisposition to function in a priestly manner, while others are inclined by these same factors to be prophets. Obviously we should develop our native potentials. Yet we need also to keep a balance. Otherwise we may distort the use of these native endowments. The result will be another instance of polarization between two emphases that belong together.

Once we become unbalanced we become defensive when confronted with the necessity for the other emphasis. This defensiveness in turn tends to sustain the polarization. The fact remains, however, that priests function better as priests when they function also as prophets, and prophets function better as prophets when they function also as priests. Perhaps the best way to illustrate this point is to see the balance in action in the ministries of specific individuals in our ecclesiastical tradition and to note the effect of their ministries upon those to whom they ministered.

Paul's Ministry to Philemon

The first illustration is the caring of Paul for Philemon as recorded in his letter to Philemon. He wrote this letter as an intercession for a runaway slave named Onesimus whom he had come to know and to love. The slave's master was Philemon to whom Paul had ministered in times past in a priestly way. He does not hesitate to use this priestly rapport to function as a prophet to Philemon. "I want some benefit from you in the Lord," he said.

Though he was sending Onesimus back to Philemon, his purpose was to change the structure of their relationship. Receive him back, he wrote, "no longer as a slave but as a brother." It was more than a simple request. Paul's priestly caring for Philemon had given him the right also to insist. "You owe me," he said, "even your own self."

While we have no account of what followed in the relationship between Paul and Philemon, it is possible that Paul's prophetic challenge to Philemon may have opened the way for another priestly opportunity. Since one of the reasons for our reluctance to exercise the prophetic ministry is our concern about the reaction of those to whom we minister, the prophet who is also a priest hopefully will communicate the sensitivity that enables people to express not only anger but also fear. Although the natural inclination is to react toward a hostile response with some hostility of our own, our priestly sensitivity may be sufficient to move us instead to detect the anxiety behind the hostility. When we respond to the hostility with acceptance, we are making it possible for the other to express his underlying fears. Perhaps Philemon may have been concerned about the precedent he might be initiating in treating a slave as a brother.

Beside the courage to be prophetic we need also the compassion to be priestly. People are more likely to confront their fears if their natural resistance to the prophetic approach is not pushed into open defiance. The prophet who is most likely to effect change at the deeper levels of human motivation is the one whose attitude encourages others to engage him openly in dialog.

John Woolman's Ministry in Colonial America

An illustration of this balance in action from American church history is the ministry of John Woolman as it is recorded in his *Journal*. Woolman lived during the Colonial period. A Quaker by faith, he was a tailor by trade. He also drew up wills. Like Paul he worked at his trade to raise money to finance periodic journeys to the Quaker meetings established throughout the thirteen colonies. Unlike Paul he had a wife and children whom he left behind. His desire was to strengthen the brethren in their faith and to share his faith and love for Christ.

83

As Woolman went about his priestly ministry he became increasingly disturbed by an accepted institution in Colonial society—the practice of human slavery. He could care for slaves and slaveholders as a priest—and he did—but he was aware that slavery was distorting not only the life of the slave but also of the slaveholder. How could one love his neighbor as Christ has loved him and still enslave him? Feeling constrained to act he began at the most logical place—his vocation. When people came to him to draw up their wills he began to ask them what they planned to do with their slaves. Upon the basis of the New Testament he tried to convince them to free their slaves. If he failed in this attempt at "sweet reasoning," he would try to persuade them to *will* their slaves their freedom. If he failed also in this, tears would come to his eyes and sadly he would inform them that out of loyalty to Jesus Christ he could not draw up their wills.

Soon he began to add this prophetic dimension in his priestly journeys to the Quaker meetings. In the process of comforting the brethren he would bring up the question of their slaves. With the Bible before them he would attempt to show why they should free their slaves. Then he would listen patiently to their response, always keeping the conversation as a dialog. His mission attracted other Quakers, particularly the young, who joined him in his journeys, participating in this same balance of the priestly with the prophetic.

They were so effective in this combination that before Woolman's death and one hundred years before the Civil War, the Quakers in annual meeting decided that no one could be a member of the Society of Friends and own slaves. The feat was all the more remarkable when one considers that the Quakers reach their accord by unanimity rather than by majority vote. In those days the Quakers were larger in proportion to the population than they are today. If other denominations had done half as well, it is tantalizing to speculate on the results. We just may have avoided the Civil War as well as all the unfinished business from that war still plaguing us today.

There were two alternatives to Woolman's prophetic ministry among Christians of the Colonial period. Some had so adjusted to the cultural values that they believed slavery was correct. Clergy as well as laymen not only owned slaves but attempted to justify the practice on the basis of the Bible. Others admitted that slavery was wrong. They refused to own slaves. Yet they felt the institution was too deeply rooted in the political and economic structures of the Colonies to change it. So they shrugged off their responsibility by saying, "What can you do?"

The acculturated Christians exercised their power to strengthen slavery. The "shrugging" Christians buried their talent of power in a napkin. In contrast to both, Woolman and his companions recognized the distortion in society and took the initiative to contact as many slaveholders in their fellowship as they could. They did not move beyond this fellowship and attempt to change the law governing slavery. But they did change their church! The "powers that be" did not become the democratic process until the Colonies revolted against English domination and became the United States of America. There were later moves in the direction of eliminating slavery by political action but they were not successful. The most promising of these was the efforts of some in the Continental Congress to include a prohibition of slavery in the Declaration of Independence. Unfortunately for them and for us their efforts were sacrificed to the priority of achieving a union.

The Congregation as the Environment for Ministry

The local congregation now as then is the most pertinent environment in which the balance in action can be achieved. As the "gathered group" the local congregation provides a place where the pressing issues of society can be discussed. The prophetic concern for justice and the priestly concern for healing move God's people to take seriously their obligations to these issues. While there will be differences of opinion in such discussions, there is also a point of view that they hold in common. This is why John Woolman opened the Bible on the issue of slavery. There is a standard—a Word of God— and it can and should be brought to bear on the issues at hand. The Bible does not give specific answers to the complex problems of our society, but it is the basis on which the people of God can bring their wisdom and expertise to bear on these complex problems.

To some this may seem to contradict the very purpose of the church. As one church member put it, "I want to get away from all these troubles in the world when I go to church." He has a point. We attend church as a needed retreat in which we receive comfort and inspiration to carry on. Yet a discussion of the issues of the day need not disrupt the church's ministry of comfort. The priestly ministry, one to another, is essential for those who gather together. They— we—need support for our sagging spirits and peace for our distraught minds. There is a difference, however, between a retreat in which our spirits are refreshed and one that provides an escape from responsibility. The priestly way of caring offers the support we all need to function in the midst of frustration, while the prophetic way of caring protects our retreat from degenerating into a "cop-out" from the Christian calling. With comfort we need also challenge and

86

with peace we need also confrontation. The church is in the world, though not of it. The word *church* in the New Testament comes from the Greek word *ecclesia* which means those who are *called out*. Christians are *called out* of their cultural distortions, not into them, in order to exercise their care within that culture. The life of the congregation should reflect this care.

When we think of the prophetic way of caring in the local congregation we tend to think of preaching. The pulpit is, of course, involved in both priestly and prophetic ways of caring. This does not mean that the sermon must necessarily take stands on the pressing issues of the day, many of which are controversial. But it should at least raise questions about the issues. The proclamation of the love of God in Christ cannot be confined to comfort. Nor can it be divorced from the call to responsibility.

The prophetic challenge from the pulpit can be given in a kindly spirit. The stereotype of the prophetic preacher as the hostile flagellator of his congregation is as far removed from the genuinely prophetic as from the priestly. Prophets do not have to be angry to be authentic. The need—especially in our day of rapid social change and painful alienation—is for kind prophets—priest-prophets—whose task is to reconcile rather than to polarize.

As important as preaching is, the prophetic emphasis in the congregation is best served by dialogical surroundings. Sermons that focus on prophetic issues need to be coupled with feed-back opportunities for the congregation. An increasing number of churches are having such feed-back sessions during or following the service. If they are to fulfill their purpose these sessions should permit freedom of expression. The preacher as well as those who agree with him need to face up to their natural resistance to disagreement. Once there is an openness of expression, the feed-back sessions can do much to enhance the effectiveness of the sermon.

Educational and special interest classes have a built-in dialogical basis and therefore are excellent forms for the priestly-prophetic stimulus. Study groups have a similar advantage. Forums in which the problems of the day are presented and then discussed are excellent formats for dealing with ways and means for initiating action. An appointed task force is a currently effective means for carrying out the plans. Such forces—organized around a task and dissolving when the task is completed—can be assigned to priestly as well as prophetic concerns.

Visitation committees in charge of ministering to the sick, the elderly, and the bereaved, as well as evangelism committees, best function as continuing operations of the congregation. Other priestly concerns may be met by specific group-oriented means such as marriage nurture classes or parent education courses, which have, like the prophetic task force, terminal points within which they fulfill their immediate purpose. The Alcoholic Anonymous model is a practical guide for selecting the personnel for these priestly ministries. Who knows better how to minister to the sick, the bereaved, the lonely, the lost, or the maritally troubled, than those who have been through these ordeals themselves.

In the prophetic dimension a social concerns or social action committee can also best function as a continuing operation of the congregation. Composed of people sensitive to human needs in national, state and local problems, this committee can pinpoint the issues upon which the congregation should concentrate its energies and appoint task forces to function in these areas.

It is helpful if the personnel of these forces include persons with vocational expertise in the area of the task. It has been common in our past to overlook such expertise in our congregations. For example, we utilize a person who has knowledge of the economic scene to be financial secretary of the congregation rather than to channel his knowledge into the congregation's concern for a Christian witness in the world of business and industry. Such a person in turn needs support from the congregation to function in his vocation in terms of his Christian commitment.

The local congregation is not the only church of the community. Consequently it should extend beyond itself to join with other congregations in the community in carrying out the church's priestly and prophetic mission in that community. Ecumenical endeavors not only prevent unnecessary duplications and competition, but also bring greater resources to bear for a more effective ministry. When congregations can function as clusters the lay potential for ministry in experience, expertise, and vocational power is enhanced, as is the potential for people power. Ecumenical endeavors also bear witness to the unity of the church, which helps in a sense to redeem our unfortunate history of division.

Organized caring need not be confined to local congregations or any other structure of the church as an institution. *Ad hoc* groups of God's people may gather together without the benefit of congregational support to do a job. In conversing with a local political figure who is also a Christian, I asked him how he related his Christian concerns as a politician to the work of his church. "I have a hard time with that," he said. "I don't really work with my own church when I want to get something done in the community."

When I asked why, he replied, "In politics if I get fifty-one percent of the vote I have the power to function. In the congregation even if I get a seventy-five percent majority I may not be able to get the job done. The strong minority can create too much of a problem."

"So what do you do?" I asked.

"I call certain persons I know are interested and we get together, plan a strategy, and go to work."

When I asked if these persons belong to churches, he said, "Most likely they do, but we don't think of ourselves as a church."

Of course they don't. We are too institutionally oriented for this kind of mental flexibility. Yet when God's people gather together to do a job in caring for their neighbor's needs, there too is the church.

Chapter 9

Changing History

We are living in a day of such rapid social changes that even those who normally are "with it" are finding themselves "out of it." Procedures, customs, and structures are not as fixed as in a previous day of slower change. Minority peoples have broken through traditional ways to modify the patterns of previously accepted discrimination. Students have upset the traditional educational structures to alter the patterns of student-teacher relationships. In many institutions they have significantly changed the educational process. A counter culture is emerging that challenges traditional values and customs.

Too Much Responsibility

This widespread and rapid change has created a problem. People become victimized by it, and suffer from what Alvin Toffler has popularized as "future shock." Literally overcome by the proliferation of diversity, we are faced with decisions which used to be at least partially made for us by the accepted cultural values and social mores. This increase in freedom has not always been in line with our desires. The greater responsibility that it entails is frightening.

In defense some have resisted not only the changes but the very idea of change itself. Such resistance is illustrated by a letter to a magazine editor in which the writer expressed the hope for a new edition of Horatio Alger. "Then we will be well on the way to restoring the sanity of our young."

The writer was looking backward for a symbol of the America that was instead of ahead to the America that is being shaped by the current changes. The accepted symbols of yesterday's culture seem more in our age to caricature ideals than to communicate them. Looking backward for support leaves us more unprepared for the changes of the future.

Opportunity to Influence Change

A day of change is also a day of opportunity to influence change—to manage it. For the church this means the opportunity to change rather than to repeat its ecclesiastical history. "History repeats itself" is the familiar cliche, but historians Will and Ariel Durant say otherwise. "There is no certainty that the future will repeat the past; every year is an adventure" *(The Lessons of History,* p. 88).

If adventure is the potential for every year, how much more is it for our present era when traditions no longer block the way for change. Despite their value in providing a continuum for the past into the present, traditions can also predispose the present to be merely a repetition of the past. When nothing new can enter because of tradition, human freedom and spontaneity are thwarted. Today the most fixed positions of the past are being questioned—for good or ill. The changes in Roman Catholicism initiated by the Second Vatican Council are an example of what is happening generally to traditions. The guardians of tradition may still attempt to reinforce their sagging authority, but the winds of change continue to blow. Interpretations of ancient beliefs are now being offered that would scarcely be entertained in a more stable era.

In the realm of values those who would have been considered losers in a former age are now feted as winners. Previously it was expected that one would stay at a job before he could instruct others on vocation, or that he would need to make a "go" of his marriage before he could be an authority on marriage or its facsimiles. Such expectations are no longer the case. What once was considered failure may now be interpreted as emancipation. What before was considered "messing up one's life" may now be put forth as an alternative life style. There is a whole new set of criteria for accepted values. Few of our previously assumed cultural supports for the so-called good life remain.

Such shaking of our traditional foundations has had its destructive results in the lives of those who have been unable to accept the growing demands for personal responsibility. It has also had its constructive influence in making change possible in situations that had been locked in by traditions. The church's imbalance in caring is a pertinent example. The possibility of joining the concerns for the individual and for the social context in one balanced ministry— a priestly-prophetic balance is now more realistic.

The tenuous relationship of the church to social context in the world has also been an obstacle to achieving this balance. Though "in the world," the church is not "of the world." Because of this tenuous relationship to the world, Christians have continually been tempted to withdraw from it rather than become involved in it. Many have seriously questioned the wisdom of spending much of their energies in trying to improve it. The gap between the cultural values and those of the kingdom of God is so great that involvement in the world is not only useless but hazardous.

An Obstacle to Effecting Change

This tenuous identification of the Christian with the world has its counterpart in the Christian's need to be "ready" when the Lord returns. So convinced was Paul, for example, that Christ's return was in the near future that he advised the Corinthians to make no change in their current status in the world. If they were married, stay married; if single, stay single; if a slave, stay a slave—"for the form of this world is passing away" (1 Cor. 7:31).

When the Thessalonian congregation took his predictions of the second coming too seriously—some may have even ceased to work in the anticipation or the event—Paul insisted that they had misunderstood: the second coming was not yet since several signs were still to be revealed (cf. 2 Thess. 2). Therefore, they were to carry on with their duties in the world. But the implication is still clear: while Christ's coming for Paul was "not yet," it was also "not far off."

Fourteen hundred years later another leader of the church in the beginning of another era of history felt the same way. Martin Luther believed as Paul that Christ was coming soon. There was little purpose, therefore, in long-range planning. Apply first aid to the sores and problems of society, of course, but time was too short to undertake any fundamental changes to eliminate the causes for the sores.

Obviously he was wrong as was Paul before him. Christ did not come in the near future, and later generations have suffered at least indirectly because of their sureness. As George Forell put it *(Faith Active in Love.* Minneapolis:

Augsburg, 1954, p. 163), "It must also be granted that Luther's unrealized expectations of an immediate end of the world resulted in an unnecessarily superficial repair of the social structure of this world. It does make a difference whether one is going to inhabit a house for another month or another year."

This sense of the imminence of Christ's coming has blocked not only Paul and Luther but many other church leaders in the development of their prophetic way of caring. Jesus himself is on record as stating that he did not know when he would return—that only the Father knew. He did, however, say it would be *soon,* and he described the signs that would precede his coming. The problem is that there have been those in each generation who have identified the signs— wars, rumors of wars, famines, earthquakes, persecutions— and predicted his imminent coming. Such anticipation has moved people to be prepared for his coming; it has also moved them to be unprepared in the event that he did not come.

We see the same disinterest in the world today among the Jesus People. A recent study of one of the communes of this movement discovered that the majority of these young people listed themselves as previously being radical or liberal in their political activity. After joining the movement, however, they no longer care about the political scene. In attempting to account for this change, those who made the study said, "We asked them how one could change society if he took no part in politics, and they gave us replies consistent with religious fundamentalism. 'The only way to change society is to change men's hearts,' said one. 'Politics is man's way not God's way, and it has failed,' said another" ("Jesus People," *Psychology Today,* Dec. 1972, p. 110).

The secular counterpart to this stance toward society is

espoused by those whose pessimism regarding the human scene is based more on negative experiences than on religious faith. Having a cynical attitude toward all human institutions including government, they see no hope of changing society. Investing any time and effort into programs for effecting change, therefore, is a waste of time. Rather than saying the time is too short, they say, it won't do any good. The effect, however, is the same.

Being ready for the Lord means not only being ready for his coming, but also ready should he delay. The familiar patchwork on societal evils needs to be accompanied by long-range efforts at change. The symptoms need treatment but so also do the causes. Priestly caring needs to be accompanied by prophetic caring. Some examples of this balance are as follows:

Priestly Care	*Prophetic Care*
Feed the hungry person.	Seek to alleviate the institutionalized injustices and inequalities of opportunity that predispose some people to be poor.
Provide housing for a homeless family.	Labor within the political-economic structures to secure adequate housing for all.
Visit those in prison to share the reconciliation of the gospel and its sustaining strength.	Seek to change the societal injustices that predispose the poor to make up most of our jail population—the great majority sentenced without a jury trial via the plea bargaining system —while more affluent offenders manage to have their built-in loopholes.

Comfort those who have lost loved ones in war with the hope of the gospel.	Concern with the problem of war itself and the ways in which we justify any particular war in order to give meaning to the deaths it brings about.
Visit the elderly to share with them the Christian fellowship.	Seek to change the attitudes of a society that isolates its aged and deprives them of dignity and meaning.

Until we are concerned about the built-in discrepancies in education, health care, housing, and jobs that exist in our society, we are not being faithful stewards of a Christ who may or may not be coming in our near future. When our efforts in meeting our neighbor's needs are confined to emergency measures, these very measures can become obstacles to any genuine change in society. If we confine our care to first aid, we may unintentionally be helping to perpetuate the inequities in our corporate structures.

Ready Should He Not Come

To change our history we need to anticipate the future rather than to be sure there will not be one. There is a difference between being "anxious for the morrow" and being prepared for it. Those who see the signs of his imminent coming exercise a needed sense of urgency lest we over-invest in a world of passing values. One can get bogged down in the temporary, and, as the ancient collect states, can so "pass through things temporal" that we finally lose "the things eternal."

Those within the churches who do not see the signs of his imminent coming are rarely given credit for any spiritual insight. Yet they too may be exercising a needed sense of urgency lest we under-invest in a world of passing values. Despite its institutionalized evils the world is still God's world. So let us not underestimate its importance or we will be poor stewards of our power to effect change in it.

Although Luther was hindered by his certainty of the imminent coming of Christ from investing himself in anything long-range in the improvement of society, he had the right idea of its importance. To him it was God's kingdom on the left hand, compared to God's kingdom on the right hand which is in heaven. We belong to God's kingdom on the right hand by believing in him. But faith in God is not confined to times of prayer or public worship or talking with others about God. Rather it is a powerful influence upon our total life in the world. Our faith works through love (Gal. 5:6). To whom is this love directed? To our neighbor in the kingdom on the left hand. It is directed toward meeting his needs.

Since our society with its people and its structures for living together is the scene in which love does its work, the need is for wisdom in the expression of this love. We are not likely to achieve this wisdom if we are confined in our efforts to emergency measures. The Christian concept of readiness means readiness either way—readiness if he comes and readiness if he does not. The double readiness frees us to direct our efforts to the deep-rooted injustices in the structures of society and at the same time enables us to accept failure in this effort since our security is in our involvement in the kingdom on the right hand—in our unconditional acceptance as persons by God through Christ.

If we are liberated to work for change in the future we can also invest our efforts in the diminishing if not preventing of "future shock"—and future generations in shock. Being prepared should he delay his coming is no less an act of faith than being prepared should he come. Or to put it another way, trusting in God is not the same as being irresponsible stewards.

As responsible stewards we need to take stock of our efforts as individuals in our specific vocations, as local congregations, as larger church bodies, or as informal groups of Christians concerned about specific needs. How should we proceed in our expression of love in each of these dimensions of activity if the world were to last another one hundred, five hundred or five thousand years? In other words, how can we alter the course of our ecclesiastical history so that we can accomplish in the future what we have not in the past, a balance between the priestly and prophetic ways of caring?

If God's will is to be done on earth, as it is in heaven, his priests need to become prophets without ceasing to be priests; and his prophets need to become priests without ceasing to be prophets.

Chapter 10

52175

Developing Your Own Model

Although we have attempted to establish the necessity for a balance of the priestly and the prophetic ways of caring, we have given the major portion of our attention to the prophetic way because it has been largely neglected. The emphasis on changing persons rather than society has dominated our ecclesiastical history. A changed person, it is hoped, will become a change agent in society.

An Uncharted Ministry

It has been said repeatedly that "the only way to change society is to change the hearts of individuals." The person with the changed heart, however, is given no maps or directions or models or plans by which he is to function as a change agent. There should be no mystery, therefore, that Christians have effected so little change in their society. In fact, though they are well disposed and well meaning, they may not even recognize the problems.

In my community an Urban Coalition is promoting a play dealing with white racism entitled *The Man Nobody Saw*.

101

In the words of the president of the coalition, it is aimed at the white majority, specifically, "those with the responsibility for the conditions and the power to correct them, those essentially humane and compassionate people who are too often silent about their convictions and far too often unaware of the social impact of their actions."

The church has not left its priestly way of caring so uncharted. How much evangelism would take place without plans and programs? Where would Billy Graham be without the Billy Graham organization with its expertise in the programming and administering of mass evangelism? In their concern for personal evangelism many congregations are using the Kennedy Plan with its specific format and procedures. The results claimed for the program indicate that some plan for evangelism is needed if evangelism is to take place.

Nor do churches leave the ministry of pastoral care to the good intentions of Christians. Rather there are training sessions and courses for pastoral visitors and pastoral counselors in recognition of the skills that are needed for this ministry. There is further recognition that organization is necessary not only for teaching these skills, but also to bring those who have the skills together with those who are hurting.

The same sort of programming and planning is necessary also for the prophetic ministry. Otherwise—as with evangelism and pastoral care—the chances are poor that it will be carried on to any appreciable degree. Where there are no handles to take hold of, no practical approaches with which to get started, no companions in the task to give support, no program by which to evaluate our efforts, Christians tend to slip into silence and inaction and may no longer even recognize the needs.

The prophetic way of caring cannot be confined to a one-to-one witness. The corporate structures are the determining factors in matters of social justice, and, therefore, need to be ministered to directly. The issue about which the Urban Coalition was concerned—white racism—is a case in point. Our societal structures have a built-in racist quality. Unless these are changed, the prophet's ministry to individuals as individuals in an attempt to overcome racism is like trying to keep a leaking boat afloat by emptying it with a cup. We need the skills of community organization to effect change in our corporate structures. To help meet this need Action Training Centers sponsored by churches have come into being. Their purpose is to sensitize and educate lay persons and clergy in the prophetic ministry.

Prophetic Assist to Evangelism

The prophetic emphasis is helpful to the ministry of evangelism. In their zeal to give others the Good News, evangelists too have often failed to listen. Consequently their Good News has not been received as Good News. Many of the poor in our land and throughout the world are bitter toward the church. They view it as simply another institution in society that is exploiting them. As our urban centers become increasingly populated by the poor, the prophetic ministry is assisting the church to "get the message." The object of our evangelism concern is saying something to *us:* "You can't reach me as an evangelist unless you care about the social context in which I feel trapped, and are willing to share your advantages in that context so that I can have the same opportunities."

We cannot share the gospel of Jesus unless we are also ready to share our societal privileges. Otherwise we will reenforce the already dangerous polarization. We cannot evangelize the oppressed when we bear the image of the oppressor, even though our role in oppression is passive and indirect. Those who are silent about the injustices of society are placed in the same category as the oppressors by the oppressed.

The prophetic ministry influences the ministry of evangelism to create a dialogical medium when otherwise it would tend to be monological. "Listen to me," says the subject of our concern. "Help me with my frustrations as I see them and I will listen to your good news. For in helping me where I feel my hurt, you have already begun to be good news."

Examples to Stimulate Planning

We have pointed to the need for a plan of action in both the prophetic and priestly ways of caring. The location of a congregation, its size, and the cultural orientation of its people, are all determining factors in the kind of prophetic caring it may develop. Each congregation, or cluster of congregations, ought to develop plans of action based on careful assessment of challenges and resources. What others are doing, however, can provide stimulation.

A large downtown church in a metropolitan setting made a thorough assessment of opportunities in its immediate geographical area. The result is that the church has entered into cooperation with a downtown hospital to provide "meals on wheels" to the large number of aged people who populate the low cost apartments in its surroundings. The church made the survey of these apartments that determined this need and supplies the volunteers who deliver the meals prepared by the hospital under the direction of its dietician. The by-product of this delivery system is the daily personal contact that these volunteers provide for these lonely people—a ministry as significant as the food they bring.

A suburban church whose resources include members with experience in the political process has developed a plan of action by which the pressing local and national issues are regularly researched and the data presented to the congregation. When pertinent issues are before local, state, or national governing bodies the congregation at its worship service takes a vote concerning a particular position and sends the result to the respective governing authorities.

A small rural congregation which by all statistical evidence should be experiencing the demoralization that often goes with declining membership is instead enthusiastic and alive. The pastor has offered the following explanation. A family in the area in which both parents and children are mentally retarded was seemingly no longer able to function as a family. As a result the county welfare department was prepared to take the children from the parents. The mother and two of the daughters were being sexually exploited by persons in the community with all of the negative consequences.

Some of the members of the congregation who knew of their plight went to the welfare department to intercede for the family. The department agreed to their request to give their congregation a chance. Since then the people have "adopted" the family, enveloping them in a caring community. This involvement has revitalized the congregation and the family is prospering.

An interchurch agency long concerned with the poor has pioneered a prophetic ministry to young people within correctional institutions which is curtailing the rate of recidivism. The program attempts to bridge the gap between the institution and the community into which the young person is released. The agency selects a congregation in this community and organizes its youth to visit the youth in question while he is still in the institution. Several such visits take place to establish the relationship. Then when the youth is released the young people of the church, both as a group and as individuals, continue to surround him. In this way they assist in the difficult adjustment of an offender to his community.

Individual Christians may carry out a prophetic ministry in cooperation with institutions other than the organized church. A middle-aged couple, for example, in cooperation with the local probation office regularly assumes responsibility for youthful offenders and their families. Having reared a family of their own they are now utilizing their wisdom in establishing relationships with other children.

Denominations organize divisions, commissions, or departments to produce plans and programs. In the prophetic dimension my own denomination has an Office of Research and Analysis. Its task is to research and analyze issues of prophetic concern and to advocate specific positions and policies to the church. In this respect it speaks to the church rather than for it.

The challenge of this office as with all denominational departments is to relate its work to the congregations of the church. Ways and means are still to be devised that will assist the commission in listening to the concerns of the congregations and also to share with them the results of its research and its prophetic stance.

The Search for Structure

Most institutions today, including the church, are engaged in radical changes in organizational structure. With the winds of change has come the opportunity to change what before seemed unchangeable. Although organizational forms are necessary, there is no sacredness about any specific form. Each can become dated and obsolete.

As necessary as they are, organizational forms are a means to an end. Our present preoccupation with altering our forms has within it the danger of confusing these means with the ends. Each organizational change takes an inordinate amount of the institution's time and energy. We may so exhaust ourselves getting our own house in order that we never get to the purpose for which this order is constituted. The concentration of our efforts in changing the structures of the institution may be diverting us from putting much effort into changing the structures of society. Even retaining the old forms of institutional organization would be preferable to this possible subterfuge.

In addition to what was previously stated about the neglect of the prophetic way of caring, there is a degree of neglect also in the priestly way. Many in our congregations have experienced the pains of loss and estrangement and have come to grips in a positive way with the meaning of their faith in respect to their hurts. Yet only a comparative few of these potential priests are used by the church in its organized ministry. Thus there is a need for training programs and task forces to use these people, to learn from their experiences, and to translate their ideas into action.

Hopefully this book will be a stimulus toward these ends.

Date Due

OCT 26 '76			
DEC 18 '77			
MAR 22 '79			